THE CARE AND FEEDING
OF BOOKS OLD AND NEW

THE CARE AND FEEDING OF BOOKS OLD AND NEW

❧

A Simple Repair Manual for Book Lovers

MARGOT ROSENBERG

AND

BERN MARCOWITZ

THOMAS DUNNE BOOKS

ST. MARTIN'S PRESS ❧ NEW YORK

THOMAS DUNNE BOOKS.
An imprint of St. Martin's Press.

www.stmartins.com

Book design by Fritz Metsch

Library of Congress Cataloging-in-Publication Data

Rosenberg, Margot.
     The care and feeding of books old and new : a simple repair manual
for book lovers / Margot Rosenberg and Bern Marcowitz.—1st ed.
          p. cm.
     Includes bibliographical (p. 149) references and index.
     ISBN 0-312-30067-0
          1. Books—Conservation and restoration—Handbooks, manuals, etc.
J. Marcowitz, Bern. II. Title.

Z701 .R66 2002
025.8'4—dc21

                                                              2002072055

First Edition: October 2002

1 3 5 7 9 10 8 6 4 2

POTEMKIN
Founding Dog of Dog Lovers Bookshop

CONTENTS

CONTENTS

INTRODUCTION

When we decided to open a bookstore devoted to the literature of dogs, we discovered that dogs and books have much in common. Each has a head, a tail, and a spine. Both need good homes and loving care.

Humans have had dogs longer than they've had books. We had dogs long before we owned a bookstore and came to bookselling by an accident that in itself was related to dogs.

It was a February morning early in the 1990s, the anniversary of the death of our adored German short-haired pointer, Potemkin. As we have tried to do each year on that day, we remembered his life, not his death, and a book of dog quotations we had come across prompted a conversation that went something like this:

Bern: I wonder if there's a bookstore devoted to books about dogs.

Margot: We could find out.

Before dark that day we had an answer (there were only out-of-print dealers and catalog companies devoted to dog books) and new careers (complementing Bern's in the travel industry, and Margot's in publishing). As we envisioned it, the shop would sell both new and out-of-print books, emphasize small presses and oddball titles, and be run as if Potemkin were in charge. As we later wrote of him on our Web site, "Po had the highest ideals of any individual we've ever known: to watch him was to see something done well, with flair, with grace, with absolute goodness. He was also very funny, and he adored dachshunds. At DLB [Dog Lovers Bookshop] we refer to him as our Founding Dog." Po's example would be our standard and inspiration. Appropriately, he became Founding Dog even before the business was established. The next day we decided to call it Dog Lovers Bookshop.

A little more than a year later, our shop opened in midtown Manhattan. We were the owner-managers, stock persons, catalogers, buyers, cashiers, packers, shippers, and sweeper-uppers. Our staff consisted of two dachshunds. Elegant and intense, Ms. Rose Dackel worked as director of research and development, sacrificing many hours that might have been spent hunting for lost tennis balls and the elusive urban badger. Joining Rose was her cousin and sweetheart from puppyhood, Ch. Abelarm's Herald Houdini. A jolly slob who lived down the street from the shop, Houdini served as official greeter and willing tummy-rubbee, with the title of director of public relations.

As we acquired stock, we found no end of titles devoted to myriad canine subjects, including the care of dogs. As we amassed more and more books, we wanted one more: about the care of books. Not a curatorial tome or restorer's manual, but something as simple as the best commonsensical guide that we might recommend to a new dog owner: advice on routine daily care, accommodations, basic first aid.

We learned rudimentary book care while we learned bookselling, as we went along. Standard business practices and Potemkin's example directed the latter, but the former was first guided by simple housekeeping routines: dusting, straightening up, fussing here and there.

We soon noticed that although dogs commonly groom themselves, books are not self-cleaning. We were amazed how dirty books could get in New York City. Sealing the window frames and repeated dusting were insufficient remedies.

When we began to specialize in old books, with all the problems peculiar to them, superficial, garden-variety dirt was rarely the major concern. We encountered loose hinges, torn endpapers and dust jackets, frayed spines, and other defects that begged to be fixed.

Eventually we found simple ways to meet these challenges. We asked for advice: Don't bother, some advised; sign on for a lengthy apprenticeship in book arts, others opined. Both worthy recommendations in their way, but not in ours. By experiment, research, and serendipity, we soon found the middle way. We could respond to a book's needs as practical nurses, not doctors.

The more old books we acquired, the more we grew fascinated not just by the subject matter but by the intricacies of book construction and design and the frailties of books themselves, as physical entities. We learned to examine, clean, and, when necessary, gently repair each addition to our stock, often adding Mylar covers to protect fragile dust jackets or delicate boards. We discovered how to eliminate odors that cling to some old books. Our goal: to increase the value of each book, to assure its preservation, and to make it a better companion when it reached its new home. Older books, we believe, are much like older dogs, deserving extra care and attention, and they, too, make wonderful friends. (How often have we urged people to adopt older dogs! And how often have we urged people to read old books!)

We've found some fine old dog books over the years, including some rare and especially collectible volumes. We've also found receptive customers, eager to know how to care for the books they bought from us. But the book we wanted from the start, a book we would have recommended to customers over the years, continued to elude us. Until we decided to write it.

Our basic message is simple: You can do what we do to help old books recover their vitality and new books retain theirs. "Simple" is the watchword throughout this book. We won't ask you to do anything to a book that we don't do every day. We'll explain why we recommend common household products in the care and repair of books, and then describe how to use each one to tackle specific problems. Almost everything you need to get started is probably already in your kitchen or bathroom cabinets, your desk drawers, or your toolbox. On your shelves, no doubt, are books you love that are eager for your attention.

Our physical shop closed after four years, but our Internet business (www.dogbooks.com) and zeal for dog books, the older and more esoteric the better, continue.

As does our gratitude:

To our beloved friends and colleagues, standard wire-haired dachshunds Rose and Houdini. They are humor and fortitude, and constant reminders that love can best be spelled d-o-g.

To the memory of Potemkin.

To our dear customers and their dogs, to whom we dedicate this book.

THE CARE AND FEEDING
OF BOOKS OLD AND NEW

THE FRIENDS OF BOOKS

YOU, your environment, and your habits are your books' best friends. Books want sturdy level shelves and protection against dampness and direct sunlight. Books also need routine individual maintenance. You can provide basic care by using a few common household products, which we'll summarize below. We'll tell you why we use these products, and suggest a few specialized items as well. In succeeding chapters we'll describe how to use each product in specific cleaning and repairing tasks.

While our emphasis is on old books, we clean new books every day. With new books the task involves not so much cleaning as keeping clean. The colorfastness of contemporary printing, and other components, from acid-free papers to the laminate surfaces of many of today's hardcover books, simplify your tasks. Upkeep can keep new books looking new almost indefinitely.

Common Household Products
and Their Uses

❧

RUBBING ALCOHOL This is the product we use most of, and most often. It's our favorite cleaner for modern dust jackets (except those made of uncoated paper) and for laminate book covers and their edges. The latter attract an unconscionable amount of dirt, much as television and computer monitor screens do.

Rubbing alcohol should be used sparingly, with lint-free, clean cloths. Although liquid, it evaporates so quickly that it cannot penetrate surfaces very deeply.

Handle with care: Work with rubbing alcohol in a well-ventilated space; don't smoke while using rubbing alcohol, or use it near any kind of flame; store with the cap tight.

❧

CLEAN CLOTHS Rags used to be a popular dog's name. Rags used to have their own bag in every household, and it's a tradition whose passing we mourn, that no technological marvel we know of can equal.

We do not recommend the commercial cleaning cloths; some are too coarse, others are impregnated with chemicals that have no role in book cleaning.

Ideal are old flannel pyjamas, cotton T-shirts or tea towels, items that have been laundered many times and do not produce lint. In our experience, the older and softer the cloth, the better it cleans books. And the lighter the color of a cloth, the better it will serve as a guide to your progress.

Tasks performed with cloth and rubbing alcohol or petrolatum often produce quick, dramatic results. Trust your cloth, and turn it often. While working on a book, look at the cloth for signs of accumulating dirt, and turn it frequently to continue your work with a clean segment. A cloth will also show evidence that colors are not fast, usually before you can tell from looking at the book itself.

～ゝ

ERASERS Those large soft erasers sold in art supply houses or good stationers, such as the Artgum brand, are your first choice. Eraser technique calls for gentleness; paper that can be cleaned with an eraser can also be badly, and suddenly, abraded. To minimize damage, rub the soiled area only in one direction. We generally work the eraser toward the outer edge of the book. This motion also often helps in the cleanup of loosened dirt particles and other debris (such as eraser dregs and sticker residue that often can be "pushed" off the page), carrying it all easily to the edge of the book and on to oblivion.

Keep your erasers clean. Sticky sticker residue, for example, can adhere to an eraser and be deposited elsewhere next time the eraser is used. It's our habit to rub erasers briskly on clean paper before storing them. We've also cut away badly soiled parts of an eraser.

Erasing book paper is close work, requiring a sharp eye as much as patience and a delicate touch. We recommend that you approach the task as you would the removal of a fine splinter in a fingertip. Let reading glasses or a magnifier help you and, whenever possible, work in natural lighting.

SOLVENTS Petrolatum (petroleum jelly, such as Vaseline) is valuable in cleaning. A dab of this neutral unctuous substance on a soft cloth can work wonders against certain kinds of dirt on dust jackets and on some kinds of book casings. As a rule, the use of petrolatum is a first step in cleaning, followed by rubbing alcohol. Essentially odorless, petrolatum has the advantage of not adding to a book's smell quotient.

There are also limited roles for lighter fluid and nail polish remover (acetone) in certain delicate cleaning tasks.

WAXED PAPER This kitchen standby, famous for its resistance to water, grease, and adhesives, aids in mending torn pages and tipping in loose (detached) pages.

ADHESIVES We use transparent liquid plastic products intended for book repair (such as Brodart's Bind-Art) and that old standby, Elmer's Glue-All (a synthetic compound). What we rarely use, however, are the applicator tops that are usually part of such products' containers. No doubt these are excellent devices capable of delivering the desired quantity of adhesive in a controlled manner. We've found them troublesome in book repair. (So have our dogs. Indeed, a photo of one of our dogs sitting patiently with one elegant drop ear glued to Bern's trouser leg would serve as the ultimate warning against careless glue use.)

We usually apply adhesives with toothpicks, cotton swabs, slivers of cardboard, or small artist's brushes (such as a number 2 or 4). These delivery systems suit us perfectly. They restrict the work area, making it hard for you to try to do too much at once. They limit the amount of adhesive you apply and can help mop up if you find that even a little is a bit too much. And they don't clog like applicator tops.

A disclaimer: Throughout this book, we use "glue" as noun and verb far more liberally than we ever use any adhesive. We just like the word. In the descriptions of repairs and in general discussion, "glue" stands for the adhesive of your choice. The use of the word does not recommend the use of glue per se (an adhesive derived from animal products) over paste (a plant-based adhesive) or the synthetics (which we use almost exclusively).

❧

TAPE   Though we use it rarely, there are occasions when an invisible tape, such as Scotch Magic Tape, is useful. Cellophane tape, with its propensity to yellow and become brittle, is never appropriate in book repair. Once in a blue moon you may find roles for other tapes—masking, cloth, and the ubiquitous duct varieties included—but only when you are willing to alter the appearance of a book in the course of repair.

Technical specialists at 3M assured us that Scotch Magic Tape will not yellow with time or otherwise react with book paper. If you need to tape older book paper, which may be acidic, use photo and document tapes, which will not discolor or react with acidic papers.

Beware, however, of tapes marketed as "removable." They are removable, their makers claim, in *relative* terms.

On book paper, with the pressure of a book's construction, and with the passage of time, removable tape will become permanent.

❧

SANDPAPER We use the very finest grain sandpaper obtainable to fine-tune erasures. More often than not, we use not just the finest grain, but worn pieces of the finest grain. Sandpaper is not appropriate for all paper types. As a general rule, the older and thicker the paper, the more likely sandpaper will work without causing damage. Don't go anywhere near high-gloss paper stock or colored paper with sandpaper; you'll do more harm than good. We usually use sandpaper in conjunction with erasers.

Learning to get the benefit of sandpapering requires you to get a feel for the right pressure. If you do fine woodworking, you'll have some idea of what we mean. We learned by practicing on ourselves, on what we call "bookman's paw"—the kind of dry skin that laughs at our attempts at dead-cell sloughing and hydrating. If sandpaper doesn't abrade a bad patch of skin on our hands, it's safe for most book paper.

❧

MINIATURE VACUUM CLEANER We use a battery-powered, palm-size model with a long nozzle that's perfect for extracting dirt from a book's gutter and edges. It's also useful in keeping bookshelves tidy.

❧

HAIR DRYER A handheld hair dryer is useful for blowing dirt and other debris off books and in removing price tags or anything else that's glued to paper.

❧

MISCELLANY Among the indispensables are rubber bands, knitting needles, chopsticks, skewers, strips of cardboard, cotton swabs, artist's brushes, kraft paper, hydrogen peroxide, double-ply paper towels, toothpicks, correction fluids such as Liquid Paper, and, though it may sound improbable, an iron (useful in the battle against dog-ears). Don't forget good scissors. Left-handers are entitled to, and should invest in, scissors made for them.

❧

WORK SPACE A well-illuminated spot, with good ventilation and a clear and clean surface, preferably nonporous, is all you need. We like to stand during book chores. If you prefer to sit, consider your posture for the sake of your spine and the books'; it can be difficult to align a text block in its case if you yourself are not properly aligned as you work. In our experience, any place that lends itself to happy tasks, such as fussing over plants, is the place to work on books.

❧

A GOOD DOG Of course, you can clean and repair books without a dog at your side or your feet, but we don't recommend it. Dogs teach patience. Even if you've learned patience, dogs will remind you of it often and pleasantly, and there are bound to be frustrating moments in working with books when the canine refresher course is just what you need.

Specialized Products

❧

There are a few products not commonly found in the home or office that are helpful in the most basic book care and repair tasks. None is hard to obtain, or expensive. Several sources are listed in "Suppliers" at the back of the book.

❧

DRY CLEANING PAD   This soft palm-sized device is the ultraconservative, all-purpose grooming tool. Filled with pulverized Artgum (minced eraser, essentially), powdery silicon, or similar tiny particles, the nonabrasive cotton-mesh pad loosens grime and other substances and helps move them along for easy disposal. Used as directed, the pad cannot hurt a book and can be used on just about every surface except gilt and leather.

As it works, the dry cleaning pad releases a small amount of its contents. You will notice that the fine particles combine with loosened grime and accumulate on surfaces as you work. Avoid inhaling the residue and dispose of it thoroughly and carefully, vacuuming it up or brushing it into a covered waste bin.

The malleable pad, which requires no cleaning or other maintenance, can last a long time. You'll know it's time to replace it when it becomes excessively dirty or no longer releases its contents.

We'll refer to this item as a dry cleaning pad, but it's also called a document cleaning pad and is marketed under such names as ABC Dry Cleaner, Professional Cleaning Pad, and Cadie. Many people in the book trades still refer to it by the old trade name Opaline.

✤

CLEANING GEL Products such as Absorene Book & Paper Cleaner or Clean-Cover Gel, essentially an eraser in a bucket, are recommended because they leave little or no residue. In consistency, gels are a bit like rendered chicken fat; their smell is inoffensive to most people. Applied with a cloth, the gel is effective on cloth and paper covers. Always wipe in one direction, remove any excess, and allow a book cleaned with gel to dry thoroughly, preferably standing open, before shelving or continuing with repairs.

✤

BONE FOLDER These are oblong tools with rounded edges that are manufactured in bone or plastic. They can last forever. In simple repairs, the bone is useful in making a fine crease in clear polyester film, tucking in edges when gluing, and other tasks. Chances are that around the house or in your workshop you have something that you could use for these purposes. We prefer the professional bone. It reminds us of certain dog toys, and we like unity among the species.

✤

PROTECTIVE COVERINGS Easy to use and long-lasting, clear dust jackets that are manufactured to fit your books and rolls of vinyl film from which you custom-make your own covers are indispensable. They preserve paper dust jackets, protect delicate boards, and can also make books more attractive by minimizing imperfections.

✤

OTHER POSSIBILITIES You may find that the adhesive removers, specialty tapes, and other paraphernalia intended for archival use are ideal for personal and household tasks. Some of these items may help you not only with books but with other precious paper artifacts, from the children's artwork dissolving on the refrigerator door to the old family letters decaying in the attic.

Teaching Yourself to Clean and Repair
❧

The first time you clean or repair a book might remind you of the first time you brought home a puppy.

If you're sorry that there's a puddle on the carpet, remember that you might have confined the youngster to the kitchen with its impervious linoleum. In time you and the puppy will learn, and the spot on the carpet may become a shrine to that riotous first day of love.

The first part of our point is that learning book care, like raising a puppy, requires patience. More patience than dexterity, more patience than inventive skill. If you are handy in general, you will perform the simple tasks we outline in a trice; if you are inquisitively handy, you may improve on an established method or discover something useful, such as a garden herb that removes both the spot on the carpet and the smear on the dust jacket.

The second part of our point is that book care, like keeping dogs, becomes a way of life. Clean one book, and you may become obsessed when you see the improvement. Repair one frayed spine, and your satisfaction and the book's aesthetic enhancement may send you reeling.

Patience and routine should be your guides. Indeed, as

you might train a dog, teach yourself to clean and repair your books.

As you would in any new endeavor, expect a few setbacks, mistakes, and disappointments. So as you proceed, consult the mantras we recite:

1. Practice the methods we describe on an expendable book (lamentable phrase!). If you don't have one, visit a thrift shop and purchase a few books, which while contributing to a worthy charity will also provide you with basic training materials. It's the unknown cadaver theory: Just as you wouldn't study anatomy by dissecting your favorite aunt, you should not practice book repair on a volume you love.
2. Practice does not always make perfect, but it can protect against making things worse. Keep notes on your book care projects, to remind you of what worked and what didn't.
3. When doing anything to a book, be conservative, work slowly, and refer to statement number one before beginning each new task.
4. For each task, start with the simplest applicable product or method (e.g., don't reach for sandpaper until you're convinced that a simple eraser is inadequate).
5. Work on books in natural light. The sun illuminating your workplace reveals a book's problems more accurately than artificial lighting does. More important, it's possible to go too far with some methods (especially erasures); natural light is your best defense. If you

must work by electric light, you'll benefit from one hundred watts.

6. Take precautions when working with rubbing alcohol, glues, and solvents of any kind. Good ventilation is a must; smoking and other fire hazards are absolutely prohibited where book care is in progress.

7. Remember to keep your cleaners clean. You can transfer trouble much too easily, but we will not describe the times, while we were learning, that we removed a smudge from one book only to deposit it as a smear on another.

8. Work gently, and in one direction. This applies whether you're using an eraser, a gel, or rubbing alcohol on a cloth. Try to suppress the human urge to rub briskly back and forth or in ever-tightening circles; such movements work when you're scrubbing ink off your hands, not easing it off book paper. For best results, work toward an outer edge (e.g., from the hinge toward the fore edge).

9. When in doubt, do nothing to the injured or soiled book.

Like the care of dogs, book care is a learning experience. We once asked a week's worth of customers how often they bathed their dogs. Answers ranged from the casual ("whenever it's needed") to the precise ("we see the groomer every six weeks"). Then we asked the same customers how often they cleaned their books. No one had an answer, though all reacted with horror, mock to genuine.

If people were amenable, we continued to quiz them: "How often do you dust your bookshelves, and do you know how to care for the old book you just bought, which is in fine condition in spite of being the 1848 edition of Hutchinson's *Dog breaking: the most expeditious, certain and easy method, whether great excellence or only mediocrity is desired*? Do you know how to maintain the new books you've purchased?"

From this informal survey and others, we concluded that most people are surprised to learn that books get dirty, just like dogs or cars or kitchen floors. Unlike dogs and cars and kitchen floors, however, books can't be dropped off at the groomer or into the tub, cruised through the car wash, or slapped with a mop.

Here one analogy ends (with the great and obvious caveat—do not use water to clean books!) and another begins: Just as a dog is a person's best friend, a thoughtful reader is a book's best friend.

(2)

THE ENEMIES OF BOOKS

ALMOST everything, animate or otherwise, has enemies. Mammals, including booksellers and dachshunds, confront the facts of life: time, bacteria, inclement
weather, bad habits.

Books, too, have enemies. Just as the way people and
dogs live their daily lives affects their longevity and well-
being, the manner in which books are kept and handled
contributes to their survival, and ultimately to your
enjoyment of them.

Dirt and Other Removable Offenses

Dirt is much like obscenity: You'll know it when you see
it. The kind of dirt that concerns us, of course, is not protected by the First Amendment. Our book culprits are
common household dirt and grime, often aggravated by
debris-producing decay that afflicts old books, and
unpleasant smells.

There is a subjective element in defining the culprits.

As New Yorkers, we may have a tolerance for good old-fashioned grime that puts us beyond the pale. Then again, once a New Yorker discovers dirt and how too much of it in certain places imperils books (or children or dogs, for that matter), sensitivity can be outraged, efforts redirected, lives and book collections forever changed. For us, dirt on books became the obscenity. Some New Yorkers, similarly moved, have challenged the preeminence of our pigeons. We, on the other hand, decided to make first our shop, then our private libraries, and finally our customers' bookshelves safer havens for books and cleaner, better places, one book at a time.

Just as there's dirt you can see, there's dirt you can feel. If you want to wash your hands after handling a book, the book needs care. There may be pen and pencil markings, labels, price tags, or other foreign bodies on a book that, if they offend you, can be removed.

Then there is bibliosis. There you are, with your nose quite literally stuck in a book. "This book stinks!" you exclaim, but the observation is not succinct literary criticism. The book smells bad; and when a book smells bad, it can affect more than your nose; it may diminish your reading pleasure or trigger allergic reactions. Let the writer's ideas or mode of expression offend you, we believe, but never the physical book. No book need ever smell bad.

Fire and Water

✤

These are the implacable enemies of books. Vigilance against these destructive elements in your home or office is primary, beginning with fresh batteries in the smoke detector, fire extinguishers, or whatever else is recommended in your circumstances.

You can reduce the likelihood of major damage to books, or the chance of books as combustibles contributing to damage, by appropriate storage and display of your library. Accidents happen, so try not to build floor-to-ceiling bookshelves underneath the upstairs bathroom. While books may look handsome on shelves surrounding the wood-burning fireplace, the fire hazard is unacceptable.

Climate

✤

By and large, books thrive in environments that are beneficial to people. Of course, some people like heat and humidity; others seek desert dryness; the books that belong to these people need special consideration. Relative humidity exceeding 65 percent is in the danger zone for books.

Fortunately, most of us can control the climate in our homes and workplaces. Books benefit from careful regulation of temperature, humidity, and air circulation in the rooms in which they live, as well as the amount of sun that shines directly on the shelves. Try to keep books away from radiators, forced hot air vents, and other sources of heat, which can warp boards and dry leather bindings. Human habits that affect the environment are also important: Books will absorb the odors of cooking and smoking.

One of the easiest ways to protect books against an irreversible form of damage—sunning—is often overlooked. If you don't want to block your windows, curtain your books. Drape a Spanish shawl over them, or a Dahomey cloth, or anything else that matches your upholstery or strikes your fancy.

Insects, Mold, and Other Foes

We are never "alone." Around us are other forms of life that vary depending on climes and conditions. Many of these life-forms are like us in that they devour books, but their impulses are biological, not intellectual. Guard against dampness, keep up your basic housecleaning, and keep food away from books.

INSECTS Food attracts bugs, bugs eat food and, while savoring an after-dinner mint, notice that irresistible nineteenth century book glue based on choicest animal fats, and voilà—*buffet froid!*

There are insects that will eat the latest paperback novel, too. This does not mean that you should never curl up with a good book and a plate of cookies. It does mean that you never leave the plate of cookie crumbs on the bookcase overnight.

Consider the well-known silverfish. According to Webster, this is ". . . a wingless insect with silvery scales, long feelers, and a bristly tail. It thrives in dampness and darkness and lives chiefly on starches and sugars." Chemical analysis of many books will reveal savory starch and gelatin. At the head of your silverfish hit list should be *Lepisma saccharina*. Webster warns that it's ". . . found in houses and sometimes injurious to sized paper or starched clothes."

The famous bookworm, the larvae of many types of beetles, is another guest to be dreaded.

> *There is a sort of busy worm,*
> *That will the fairest books deform,*
> *By gnawing holes throughout them.*
> *Alike, through every leaf they go,*
> *Yet of its merits naught they know,*
> *Nor care they aught about them.*
>
> *Their tasteless tooth will tear and taint*
> *The Poet, Patriot, Sage, or Saint,*
> *Not sparing wit nor learning.*
> *Now, if you'd know the reason why,*
> *The best of reasons I'll supply:*
> *'Tis bread to the poor vermin.*
>
> *Of pepper, snuff, and 'bacca smoke,*
> *And Russian-calf they make a joke.*
> *Yet, why should sons of science,*
> *These puny rankling reptiles dread?*
> *'Tis but to let their books be read,*
> *And bid the worms defiance.*

As the poet J. Doraston warned, bookworms eat paper, leather, paste, and all sorts of things that you want left in pristine condition. If you see dead beetles, holes in book pages, or accumulations of what looks like paper turned to dust, take action. There is the minute book louse, too, with no wings but an appetite that spans the world of tasty books.

The world is full of exterminators and do-it-yourself bug sprays. We use neither, considering these methods overkill. Our goal is to make an environment safe for books without adding toxins of any kind. We don't, after all, want a world without insects or other so-called pests. We want to control their access to our books and reduce their effects, if and when they do get access. Most important, know what pests are active where you live and how to recognize any distinctive signs of infestation. Ask around; if a fellow book lover isn't well informed, a librarian, bookbinder, gardener, or exterminator may know what ails books in your vicinity.

A simple preventive against insects is boric acid powder. If you believe you have a bug problem, try small open containers of the powder on the shelves behind your books and elsewhere, taking care that the powder is not accessible to children and pets.

If you suspect insect infestation, try our favorite remedy: freezing. It doesn't poison the environment or endanger people or pets. And it's harmless to books.

Carefully wipe the affected books, taking care that they are absolutely, utterly, completely dry. Wrap them securely in plastic, which itself must be completely, utterly, absolutely dry. You can use kitchen plastic wrap or new plastic bags, wrapping books individually or in multiples. Put the plastic-wrapped books in the freezer for a day or two. Freezing turns larvae black; if present, they will be small, mean-looking, rodlike nastinesses when you unwrap the books. Leave the larvae alone for a few days, giving them time to dry out. (You can leave the affected books closed while the larvae dry.) When dry, the larvae can be brushed away without leaving smudges.

MOLD Mold is another enemy of books. Webster describes it as ". . . a downy or furry growth on the surface of organic matter caused by fungi, especially in the presence of dampness." The dry cleaning pad is helpful against mold and its effects.

RODENTS Rodents also like books. In our New York City bookshop in old and frankly ratty premises near the Empire State Building, we had mice. Most were discreet; there were a few who were boisterous (we don't know whether we or they were poor hands at Morse code, but in four years we decoded only seven words from the rapping in the baseboards). We will always believe that the mice who rapped were the ones who ate our coloring books. They never ate anything else. We repeatedly moved the coloring books, and the mice ate them in each successive location. Retailers expect a certain amount of wear and tear on stock, but eventually we lost patience and baited humane traps. We were pleased to discover that, in addition to coloring books, the mice enjoyed our homemade whole-grain dog biscuits, which we served with the traditional cheese tidbits and bottlecaps full of fresh water. All captured mice were relocated, which made for nice country outings for all of us.

Mouse droppings or other rodent indicators anywhere near books are red flags you must not ignore. If you have a rodent problem, get a dog. A good ratter is effective, environmentally sound, and will provide you with both pest control and love.

Bad Manners

There are still people who, no doubt unconsciously, wet a finger on their tongues to make page-turning easier. This appalling act transfers moisture, and worse, to the page. The book will rarely be damaged, but the next person to turn the page may come away with more than information or entertainment. Therefore, a few germ-related courtesies never hurt.

If you accidentally sneeze or cough into a book while you're browsing in a shop, it might be nice to buy the book. At the very least, confess your error to the nearest sympathetic clerk, who may have a box of tissues and a lozenge for you, and suggest that the book be kept out of circulation for a day or so.

If you sneeze or cough into a book at the office or at home and are concerned about infecting others, remove any moisture, wrap the book in plastic, and freeze it overnight.

Notes on General Household Cleaning
⋎

The manner in which you conduct basic household chores has an impact on your books. If you use a vacuum cleaner with handheld attachments, beware of using these on books. What you remove from blinds or baseboards does not belong on your books. Even a dedicated attachment, free of grime and other elements, will have too much oomph behind it. The power of the average vacuum cleaner can dislodge weak portions of an old spine, and the attachment itself, even a seemingly fine brush, can erode delicate spines and edges, leading to further breakdown. If you must use a standard vacuum cleaner attachment (such as a dusting brush, upholstery wand, or crevice tool) for book cleaning, consider enclosing the attachment's head in a thin sock, an untreated shoeshine mitt, a length of cheesecloth, or a lint-free rag. A twist-tie or rubber band can hold the makeshift arrangement together.

Consider a small hand vacuum cleaner; we use one that's battery-powered and has a long thin nozzle ideal for removing accumulations from book edges and gutters without the risk of abrasion. Once again, books get extra protection if you slip an old sock or fasten lint-free fabric over the nozzle.

A hair dryer can also be used effectively and is especially useful on decorated boards, rough-cut edges, or any fragile element. If you're hesitant to touch some part of a book, the airflow from a hair dryer may be your best choice for superficial cleaning. Choose the lowest heat and airflow settings. Remember, you're not drawing dirt up as with a vacuum cleaner; you're blowing dirt into your environment. When we use this method, we take books out on the terrace, and direct the dirt into planters, or we hold the books over the bathtub, where any accumulation can be washed away.

For routine cleaning—cursory dusting of the top edges of books and their immediate neighborhood—nothing beats the old-fashioned clean cloth. Our ideal cloth comes from 100 percent cotton fabric, laundered dozens and dozens of times. Another useful item is an old clean cotton sock, worn on the hand like a puppet. An untreated shoeshine mitt also works well.

Proper book care entails the prudent cleaning of bookshelves. What your bookshelves are made of affects how you maintain them. That maintenance affects books as well as shelves.

For book-friendly accommodations, consider shelves of glass, metal, or other nonporous finishes. To clean shelving of this type, you can do without the kinds of products that leave residues, which can adhere to and react with books. Unstained wood is another good choice for books, but remember that all wood, like any porous material, can absorb moisture, one of the great enemies of books.

If your shelves require the use of cleansers or oil-based polishes, use them sparingly and as infrequently as possible, and with the books out of harm's way. You can, but should not, make quick work of the task by moving along a shelf of books with a rag saturated with lemon oil in one hand, while the other hand raises books just enough to let you swab the shelf. Take a little more time, clear the shelf, clean it, and let it dry, preferably overnight. Your books will last longer, and remain free of the smell of wood cleaners and polishes.

Whenever you clean any surface on which books rest, be sure that those surfaces are as dry as the proverbial bone and impeccably free of residue before you return books to them.

If you do your books only one favor, let it be this: Dust them at least every six months.

(3)
CLEANING

To clean books, you need patience, common household products, and simple methods. Thus we define book cleaning 101. For specialized tasks, such as treating leather bindings, you may want purpose-made products and a bit of practice, too.

How often do books need cleaning? Only your level of dirt tolerance can answer that. If your tolerance is high, we urge that you make exceptions for older books, whose lives are prolonged by routine care. Leather bindings, for example, appreciate care that reflects special circumstances, such as an unusually dry climate.

When we finish reading a book, we clean it before shelving it. Clean books make for cleaner spaces in which to live and work.

Dust Jackets

❧

Evolved during the nineteenth century and not common until the 1920s, dust jackets are often beautifully decorative paper protectors of hardcover books.

Sometimes called dust wrappers, jackets are by definition removable and many have been removed—permanently, either discarded by choice or lost through damage or carelessness. The absence of a dust jacket on a book issued with one not only leaves the book vulnerable to wear but also reduces its value and collectibility.

Dust jackets bear the brunt of book handling and wear, collecting fingerprints, grime, residue of food and drink. They tear, wrinkle, and fade.

❧

OVERALL DIRT To remove overall dirt and fingerprints, improve a dull and dingy appearance, and reduce that unpleasant sticky feeling: Use rubbing alcohol on a clean cloth all over a coated dust jacket, including the flaps that wrap around the book's covers. A modern jacket whose surface looks and feels slick is the one that is ideal for a simple alcohol cleaning. On a plain paper jacket, use an eraser gently, always moving the eraser in one direction. The dry cleaning pad is the most reliable choice if you suspect that colors are not fast.

In our specialty, the plain paper dust jackets of such classics as the novels of Albert Payson Terhune and the *Famous Dog Stories* series published by Grosset & Dunlap are prized for their evocative artwork. In cleaning these and similar jackets, be careful to prevent the colors from running, especially the reds.

Some books, especially older ones, are jacketed in often fragile tissue- or glassine-like paper. As a rule, these are best cleaned with erasers, if at all.

❧

DIRT SPOTS To remove a concentrated dirt spot: Start with an eraser on any dust jacket. Certain kinds of sticky grime will loosen and move, but not separate readily from the dust jacket's surface. You can, in effect, corral the sticky spot to the edge of the jacket, and work it onto your fingertips for easy disposal. If the dust jacket has a coated surface, you can alternate rubbing alcohol with the eraser, loosening grime and swabbing it up bit by sticky bit with an alcohol-soaked cloth.

But beware the dreaded clean spot! Some plain paper jackets can fool you. They absorb grime so uniformly that cleaning a fingerprint may reveal a jacket of another color. Test on an inner flap or the back cover before committing yourself to massive erasures.

❧

FOREIGN BODIES To remove foreign bodies: If you have a dust jacket to which a wad of chewing gum or other matter adheres, try the deep freeze. Enclose the jacket in a plastic bag and chill it. Chewing gum is among the substances that contract in cold, making removal as easy as a flick of a fingernail or light application of rubbing alcohol on a cloth.

To safeguard these paper guardians, consider adding clear jackets (see pages 101–5.).

✧

SUN DAMAGE What can't be helped: There's no remedy if a dust jacket is faded. (The term *sunned* is used to describe the condition, which often results in dust jackets with spines of a dramatically different appearance than that of the rest of the jacket.)

The Book Proper
✧

There are technical distinctions between adhesive-bound and case-bound books. Adhesive-bound books use glue to hold the pages or groups of folded pages (called signatures) together. (The pages inside the book are often called the text block.) There are three basic types of adhesive binding: perfect, notch, and burst. In perfect-bound books, the folded ends of the signatures are *cut off* and roughened, then glue is forced into the spine and the spine is then adhered to a wraparound cover. This is the normal paperback book binding. The second and third adhesive bindings are very similar to each other. In notch binding, the *uncut* signatures are notched at the folded end and the spine is roughened, then glue is forced into the spine and notches. In burst binding, the *uncut* signatures are perforated near the folded edge and the spine is roughened, and, again, glue is forced into the perforations and the spine. Notch and burst bindings can be used for hardcover as well as paperbound books, but the hardcover versions are cheap imitations of case-bound books.

In case-bound books, the signatures are sewn together

with thread for strength and are not held together by glue alone. A hinge of strong gauze is attached to the uncut signatures of the spine with glue and is usually covered with lining paper. The hinge sticks out slightly on either side of the spine; this allows it to be attached to the boards and endpapers. Endpapers of heavy-duty paper are glued to the beginning and end of the sewn signatures. The case consists of two stiff boards (usually made of cardboard) and a flexible spine (the top of the spine is called the "head" and the bottom is the "tail"). The flexible part is then glued to the lined gauze on the spine, and the endpapers on the bound signatures are glued to the boards. The ends of the hinge are glued between the boards and the endpapers. This differs from paperback books in that the cover of a paperback is attached only at the spine, whereas the case-bound book is attached at the spine and the boards. Think of it as the difference between custom-made and mass-produced. Books made by all methods get dirty, of course; it's only in repairs, however, where how a book is made can make a difference in how it should be fixed.

Cleaning the book proper entails the care of the rigid covers and spine (and its parts). Paper-covered or fabric-covered boards or boards covered in a combination of these materials are the most common bindings today, and have been for decades. The dry cleaning pad is the ideal cleaner. Give the pad a little squeeze or twist to release some of its contents. Then rub the pad on the area you want to clean. You may rub gently, or you may exert pressure, and you may work in any direction. Carefully dispose of any residue.

⌁

LAMINATES   To clean laminates: Laminate book covers and spines can be cleaned successfully with rubbing alcohol.

⌁

LEATHER   To clean leather: Books bound in hides (such as calfskin), whether partially or fully bound in hide, are sensuous entities. These books are always a joy to handle, and when they need cleaning, the results can be remarkable, reviving not only the leather but also the subtleties of workmanship rarely seen in modern books.

When handling leather-bound books, first wash your hands. While the natural oil of human hands may be good for the leather, the dirt on our hands is not.

Supplies from the archival and library supply houses are best for leather care. There are gels to clean leather, and others to restore its suppleness. Don't be surprised if cleaning a leather binding changes its color. We have begun to clean many an old book bound in what appeared to be black leather, only to be delighted by the emergence of deep blue and green bindings.

If you have only a few leather-bound volumes, by all means try whatever leather-care product you may have around the house for your handbags or briefcases or boots. Follow product instructions.

Do not use erasers, cleaning pads, or solvents on leather.

Overly dry leather can over time degenerate and flake; this condition is called red rot. Leather suffering from red rot melts away under the gentlest cleaning pressure, scattering flakes like falling leaves, and its dyes run. It's best not to clean such a book; see chapter 5 for suggestions on protecting books with dissolving bindings.

Suede is a special case. Do not oil a suede binding. Just wipe it—and handle it with clean hands!

If you are cleaning a book that is partially bound in leather, clean either part of the binding first. Cover the first section cleaned with waxed paper or scrap paper before proceeding. If leather cleaner accidentally gets on fabric or paper, wipe it off quickly and thoroughly.

꙲

GUTTERS AND HINGES To clean gutters and hinges: Take a hardcover book and open the front or back cover; the hinges are where the covers join the body of the book. Look at the exterior of the book, and note the point where the covers move.

Within the text block, the gutter is defined by the adjoining margins of facing pages. In old books that have been neglected, the gutter can hold a tremendous amount of dirt, especially deep, where the pages meet. A handheld vacuum cleaner is ideal for cleaning this part of a book safely. Turning every page and running the nozzle up and down the gutter, preferably without touching the book, are well worth the effort and time entailed. You'll remove dust and with it other elements that could contribute to a book's decline. This routine cleaning may also disclose other problems, such as tears and loose or loosening pages.

And don't forget to sniff the book, open, at the gutter. If the smell offends you, try "The Stinky Book Box" treatment outlined on pages 48–53.

Treat the hinges the same way, and note how the

hinges move. Do the covers wobble when you open them? Are the endpapers split at the hinges? The hinges may need tightening, or other minor repairs may be in order (see on pages 63–65).

You can also run a fine clean dry brush along the hinges or gutters. A brush can sometimes dislodge debris that has worked its way into a gutter over the years; further aided by tweezers, we've plucked many a dried flower petal this way.

Book Edges
ᴪ

The three paper sides (edges) of a book are the paper parts most exposed to the elements. As a result, they require careful cleaning.

Edges can fray, chip, or show other signs of general wear. Top edges seem to be particularly vulnerable. Deteriorating paper, in the form of minute particles, can enter the air, causing irritation to eyes and nose or aggravating allergies, and most of this will be generated from the top edges. Top edges tend to collect dust and debris from the environment, both promoting deterioration in the paper and sneezing and related unhappiness in people and pets.

To clean book edges: Working from the spine outward, rub a clean soft cloth along the top and bottom edges. Archival suppliers sell a specialized dry sponge that cleans and absorbs dust.

Don't neglect the book's tail, or bottom, edge. Standing on a shelf may shield this part of the book, but it can attract dust and dirt from the shelf itself. Depending on the book's overall construction, the tail edge may suffer extra wear.

If edges are badly frayed or stained, consider using the least abrasive sandpaper you can find. Wrap the sandpaper around any palm-sized object that will keep the working side flat. (Hardware stores sell flat-bottomed sandpaper blocks in a variety of sizes.) To avoid any abrasion to the book's casing and to compensate for width (no need to prepare a sandpaper block the same dimensions as the text block), open the book, hold the text block firmly in one hand, and lightly sandpaper the edge or edges in need of extra care. Remember to work in one direction, away from the spine. As always when working with sandpaper, work where the debris you produce will not end up on the rug or in the dog's bed.

❧

UNUSUAL EDGES To clean unusual edges: Not all books have uniform plain paper edges. Some are gauffred (or goffered, referring to the ridged or pleated decoration imparted by a heated tool onto gilt or silvered paper); marbled (referring to the elegant color patterns similar to the swirls of chocolate in pound cake); sprinkled (referring to the addition of color for a speckled effect, not unlike that of sprinkles on an ice-cream cone); or unopened (the fore and top edges of succeeding pages have not been cut). Rough-trimmed or untrimmed (pages are not cut to uniform smoothness) have a following among collectors and are themselves great collectors of dust. Treat all these edges with the same extra care that gilt edges merit (see pages 42–43).

We've had a few harrowing conversations about opening unopened pages. Unopened pages offend some people, who want them opened. We suspect that the same people insist on "full quarts" to get more for their money than a mere quart could ever supply, and they want every possible page made available for orthodox page-turning. But not all anomalies are deficiencies. Before slitting an unopened page with letter opener or forefinger, by all means peek: Is there any text or artwork inside? If not, please leave well enough, and someone's design, alone. Manufacturing defects are another matter. If you determine that pages are unopened in error, you can act: Return a new book to its seller for profuse apologies and your choice of refund, credit, or another copy in A-1 condition; or you can deal with the problem yourself. Most bookbinders recommend that you use a dull knife and cut outward, away from the spine. If you try to do it yourself, use one part knife to four parts patience.

Book Pages and Endpapers

~⌇~

The endpapers are double leaves, plain or fancy, that you'll see when you open a book, from the front or back. Part of the double leaf adheres to the inside of a cover, while the other part is free (free endpaper, or flyleaf).

There are printer's blanks, half titles, and title pages, but, for simplicity's sake, all the paper that is not an endpaper is just part of the text block (the book's contents). The more pages a book has, one might say, the more dirtiable surfaces there are.

To clean the text block: The eraser is your first choice. Erasers can remove most fingerprints, pencil marks, and dirt smudges.

Ink and crayon are harder to remove. See our remarks in "About Paper" (page 39) and then decide whether you want to tackle these difficult substances. By patient alternation of eraser and finest sandpaper, with frequent time-outs to assess any creeping damage to the paper, you may be able to eradicate ink and crayon marks.

If you are unable to remove ink or crayon but are still offended by it, you might be able to conceal it. Try correction fluids applied sparingly, and repeat until you can no longer see the offense.

As a rule endpapers are of a stock heavier than that on which the book's contents are printed. This may give you more leeway in cleaning.

A rule of thumb when you find an old book and buy it because someone you know will love it: Don't just thumb through it, dust it off, and wrap it up. Turn every page, because the damnedest things turn up in old books. Some of those things are fun, most are inconsequential, some may suggest a simple repair; others are execrable, and they're the ones that can give the giving of old books a bad name. Some years ago we bought, sight unseen, a carton of old children's dog stories. We had done only the most superficial cleaning when someone dropped in and asked for a title we knew to be among the new acquisitions. We produced the book, and the customer took it and her toddler to the sofa. "Oops," she said, closing the book and grimacing. It was the beloved picture book of her youth, but she was hoping for a copy without four-letter words on almost every page. We learned to vet each book, page by page, before showing it to anyone. We also learned that apparently some words are so terrible that they must not be seen, even by someone too young to read.

～

ETHICAL ERASURES There are handwritten addenda in many of the old books we acquire, and we retain far more of these than we remove. Trying to cleanse a book of its past strikes us as the ethical equivalent of turning back a pre-owned vehicle's odometer.

We erase to clean, not to edit. So we remove smudges, scribbles, or other random pencil or pen marks, vulgarities, and fingerprints. We never erase paw prints, which we find in books with amazing frequency and consider sacred.

Worth retaining for their well-known extra appeal and value are the signatures of authors or illustrators, or other persons associated with a book. Then there are inscriptions that add charm, insight, or amusement. We've come across exquisite penmanship too beautiful to obliterate, marginalia on current events or customs that touch on an old book's subject matter, and a few rib-ticklers, such as one dating from the 1920s on the flyleaf of a British novel: "Happy birthday, darling Robert, from your adoring Mother." "Robert" was crossed out, and "Harry" substituted in the same fine hand. Just as we often delight in the names of previous owners (who were they? what did they think of the book?), we developed a special fondness for

Harry, not to mention Robert, which we hope the book's next owner, and all future owners, will share.

❧

ABOUT PAPER The kind and quality of paper also affect your ability to remove from it deep pencil marks, crayon, and ink. Run your finger over the paper: What does it feel like? As a general rule, the slicker the paper, the harder it is to clean. The more paper feels like fabric—a high-quality linen, for example—the easier it is to correct more defects. Just as, in sewing, it's easier to mend a heavy knit than a sheer silk, the nap in paper gives you room to maneuver; you can lightly abrade certain kinds of paper, burnishing with an eraser, sandpaper, or both for a finished look that can often make the work site look like new.

The Art of Ungluing

❧

Labels, tape, price stickers, and anything else that adheres to paper with glue can probably be removed, as can gum and similar substances.

You can release some chemicals into your environment by using a few drops of lighter fluid or other solvent, or a formal "unglue" product, such as those that depend on heptane and are sold by art and archival supply companies.

Instead, you can use a little electricity for our favorite method of label removal. When we determine that a label will not peel away cleanly—it resists a poke at a corner with a fingernail—we plug in the hair dryer, set it on low, and direct its flow at one edge of the label. Many labels will promptly release and begin to curl; as the label retreats, guide the warm flow of air under the raised portion of the label until you have freed it entirely. A label that behaves this way, with moderate resistance, can be removed in under a minute.

Some labels hold on longer. To deal with these reactionaries, you need equal stick-to-itiveness. Aim the hair dryer at each edge in succession, moving around and around the label. If the label is on a flyleaf or other turnable surface, direct the hair dryer at the label's other side, warming it from underneath. This procedure can take time, but most labels will eventually loosen. Take advantage of the first sign of weakness: When a label edge begins to curl, keep the airflow directed at that edge until it lifts up cleanly. Never give a stubborn label a second chance: Tear or cut away part of a large label that has come away from the surface, and don't allow it to reattach to the surface while you and the hair dryer are working on another edge.

Take care not to cook the paper and the adhesives, some of which can scorch the very spot you're trying to clean. We learned this when a label did not want to be removed and we turned up the hair dryer's temperature. Keep the hair dryer on low, and take your time. If using the hair dryer sounds cumbersome, just think of it as the equivalent of removing labels from a food container by running hot water over it until the label can be scraped or peeled away. If salvaging that pickle jar is worth the effort, so is the delabeling of a book. The principle is the same.

One benefit of the hair-dryer method is that the heat can

soften many adhesives enough that they come off quite cleanly, along with the label itself. If there's gumminess where the label was, a soft eraser often scoops it right up.

On coated dust jackets and laminate surfaces: Many labels, including the modern self-adhesive variety, like to assert themselves by leaving a film or tiny bits of adhesive behind them. Tidy up with rubbing alcohol on a soft cloth.

Far more troublesome are labels added to endpapers. Some labels may come off easily and completely, but only by taking a layer of paper with them. Such abrasions—as if the paper has a mild case of shingles—can often be eased by light sandpapering, especially if the paper has a generous nap to it. The method is worth trying only on book paper that is white, of course. Proceed with caution: Leave labels in place whenever their removal might cause damage.

Some labels and their adhesives will leave a thin but brittle residue or discoloration. An eraser and fine sandpaper can work well against these blots. If they fail, try a heptane-based solvent. However, always consider the surface on which you're working: If there's nap in the paper and if the paper is white, give it a try.

Removing cellophane tape: Cellophane tape—the kind that yellows with age and has probably been replaced in most homes and offices since the advent of invisible tapes—is something you may want to remove. You may find it on an old repair that you want to improve, if only for a better appearance.

The cellophane backing should release; pull it up gently. Then blot the adhesive out of the paper; use an iron (medium-hot setting) over kraft paper.

If adhesive residue remains, other methods (such as solvents) are not recommended. A light sandpapering, if the paper is white and has a good nap to it, may minimize the adhesive scarring.

Removing modern tape: Acrylic is used more and more in the adhesives of tapes sold these days, and acrylic is here to stay: It will not blot out of paper as some older adhesives may. Even if you can remove a modern tape's backing, you may be faced with a scar that even sandpapering will not improve.

Gilt and Other Decorations
꙳

Gilt edges and stamping add special lustre to a book, and need extra care for preservation. You'll discover gilt on one or more edges, the spine, or boards, and we do mean "discover"—more than once we've begun cleaning an old book and been dazzled to see gilt emerge from the haze of grime. What Dr. John Ferriar knew in 1809, and made famous in "The Bibliomania: An Epistle to Richard Heber, Esq.," still motivates today:

How pure the joy when first my hands unfold
The small, rare volume, black with tarnish'd gold

Few of us are privileged, as Ferriar was, to exchange heroic couplets with a friend and fellow collector like Heber, whose library contained 150,000 volumes when it was disposed of in the late 1830s—but we can all know their joy.

Gold's malleability is one reason the ore is so desired. It can be processed and rolled to almost unimaginable thinness. At this weight, it has almost no monetary value, but stunning aesthetic potential.

Be extremely gentle when cleaning gilt. Wipe in one direction only, with the softest cloth available. If you wipe with a back-and-forth stroke, you risk loosening tiny particles of dirt or underlying paper and may wear away some of the gold.

Never clean gold stamping with a product that contains hydrochloric acid (found in commercial and household bleaches), even in dilute forms. Never use a product containing any amount of aqua regia ("royal water"), a mix of nitric and hydrochloric acids that dissolves gold and platinum.

Artwork, embossings, insets, and other attractions of a handsome old case will usually respond well to cleaning gel. If you are concerned about colorfastness on a pictorial board, test a corner before you undertake an overall cleaning.

A Warning About Labels

Browse through any bookstore and you'll come upon current books whose honors—Newbery, Caldecott, the Schlegel-Tieck translation prize, and others—are heralded on the dust jacket by the addition of a label. You may also come upon these in used or out-of-print bookshops.

No matter where you find books with label-added dust jackets, you will want to clean them at some point. Proceed with extra caution. That the dust jacket is appropriate for cleaning with rubbing alcohol does not mean that the label is, too, even if it looks glossy and slick. We've seen sharp black type on a shiny gold label smear into illegibility, and other labels wipe clean down to their plain-paper or adhesive layer. Do not assume that any addition is made as well as the dust jacket it adorns. Approach these additions with the dry cleaning pad.

A last label warning: Adhesives of poor quality may be used to attach these or other promotional labels, and the result can be progressively disagreeable. A peeling label is itself unsightly. The discoloration of the dust jacket caused by the label's adhesive is even less attractive. Be ready with a drop of glue at the first sign of label peel.

Stains and Foreign Objects

Many stains are, for all practical purposes, permanent: coffee on a cloth binding, most food splatters on endpapers and throughout the text block, fat-based smears, cosmetics residue, grass stains, and imprints from vegetation on any uncoated paper. Some permanent stains can be reduced by sandpapering, but this method should be limited to edges. What the eminent Cockerell wrote more than a hundred years ago is true today: "Nearly all stains can be removed, but in the process old paper is apt to lose more in character than it gains in appearance."

Chewing gum is one of the substances that contracts

when cold. Chill a book, and chewing gum should be easy to remove.

Squashed insects, if thoroughly dried, often vanish with the flick of a fingernail or a dry brush.

Nail polish and similar enamel-like substances on a high-gloss surface, including some dust jackets and most laminates, disappear at the touch of a cotton swab dampened with nail polish remover or other acetone product. Clean the work area promptly with rubbing alcohol on a clean cloth.

Rust stains: Approach these blots with sandpaper of the finest grain. Fine sandpaper that is worn, but clean, is often even better. As you proceed, slowly and patiently, watch for signs of abrasion to the paper; remember that what Cockerell wrote on the subject cannot be overemphasized. Some rust stains can be reduced or removed by gentle bleaching. Dip a toothpick's tip in hydrogen peroxide and apply it to the stain. Have handy some double-ply paper towels for any excess—this is an occasion when almost any amount of fluid is excess! Do not use peroxide on rust stains on or near type or artwork.

Library markings: It's often easy to remove a library pocket, if you don't object to the roughened area that removal usually causes. On the other hand, the pocket can be useful, by holding your bookmark while you're reading. Perforations, stamps, and other library markings are meant to be permanent, and they usually are.

Modern Paperbacks
❧

Paperbacks may not have been made to last, but to be inexpensive and portable; if they fall into the swimming pool, one can worry more about the drain than the book. But they're still books, and as books they deserve respect. Some of us are even inordinately fond of them, and some of the early paperbacks are collectible and beautiful.

Most of the cleaning procedures and caveats we've described for hardcover books and their dust jackets apply to paperbacks. If the wraps (a paperback's paper covers) are coated, rubbing alcohol will clean them. If not, proceed with caution and an eraser, treating the whole book as you would a plain-paper dust jacket.

To preserve an old paperback, consider archival-quality synthetic wrappers or bags with an acid-free backing. Remember to guard against moisture when bagging a book. To allow some air circulation, make a few pinpricks in a paperback's bag. (See pages 101–4 for more about protecting individual books.)

What Can't Be Helped
❧

ACID Some books are printed on paper with a high acid content. The acid causes the cellulose fibers in paper to break down. This causes the paper to discolor, become brittle, and sometimes even fall apart. At its worst, this type of cheap, cheap paper is found in newspapers and books produced in the United States, Britain, and other countries under wartime restrictions. Quality old books, which we have from the nineteenth and twentieth centuries, are often quite white and supple, and age well.

Nothing at the do-it-yourself level can be done to salvage books printed on high-acid paper.

⟅⟆

BROWNING   This is discoloration caused by acid content. Most book paper turns brown uniformly, so that what once was white is now beige, grayish brown, or yellowish brown. Now and then you may find a book that has browned in an almost abstract pattern. You may even find a culprit, such as paper or a bookmark (or their imprints), that has reacted with the book, leaving browned areas. Even some modern books produced inexpensively or carelessly will gradually brown, sometimes just on the edges, or progressively from the edges until each page is entirely browned.

Professionals can treat browning, but the process is expensive. Consider it only if, on professional advice, you are warned that a book is doomed without extreme treatment.

⟅⟆

FOXING   As humans grow older, they often develop skin discolorations. Old books do, too, and it's called foxing. Book paper that is "foxed" shows splotches, usually of a brownish-yellowish hue. The name, first recorded in the middle of the nineteenth century, comes from the observations that it looked as if a fox with muddy paws had trampled across the page. Foxing is usually the result of impurities in the paper. Professional book restorers can treat foxing, but may charge as much as a dermatologist would to remove comparable imperfections from your skin. The process involves unbinding the book and treating each individual leaf in deacidifying, sizing, and bleaching solutions, after which the book must be reassembled.

We long ago made our peace with foxed books. As a member of the family Canidae, the fox is part of our daily lives as specialist book dealers. We like foxes. We remember an old book, published in Great Britain around 1910, that no artist could have made more beautiful than foxing did, for the book was beautifully foxed. Its subject: hounds and horses and foxhunting. Judging from the track of muddy paws up and down the text and over the artwork's countryside, the fox escaped. A wonderful book!

WATER STAINS We know of no introductory-level cure for old water stains. For what to do when a book gets wet, see pages 74–76.

REMAINDER MARKS We have discovered no surefire way to eradicate these profound blemishes, which are usually red or black slashes or dots on book pages' bottom or top edges. Fine-grain sandpaper removes some of these marks, or leaves them less prominent. No doubt publishers have their reasons for befouling books with these marks. The result, in our view, is vandalism.

The Stinky Book Box, or the Box for Stinky Books

Turn to *Webster's* (we've just consulted the Ninth New Collegiate Edition) for the definition of "absorbing" and you'll read, in part, "fully taking one's attention." There follows an example of the adjective's use: "an absorbing novel."

For readers the definition suggests that a book is especially rewarding, enriching, informative, entertaining. To us, the meaning expands: Our attention is often "fully taken" by an old book's smell. It's an experience we do not relish, and one we try to spare our customers.

To do so, we engage in a perverse and ultimately practical ritual: We sniff books.

At least once a week we schedule a formal book sniffing, and to keep it from becoming a chore we make it a party. Indeed, what could be more appropriate? New acquisitions, wonderful old books about dogs, surround us and deserve a fitting welcome. By party time, the books have been carefully dusted, aired, and cataloged. It's as if we've all been introduced, and now it's time to get better acquainted.

We set the table with a pot of chamomile tea, a box of tissues, and a pile of books. Between us, a dachshund relaxes on the sofa.*

A book is selected and opened. We take turns poking our noses into the book's gutter. We inhale. . . .

---

*Rose's presence on the sofa requires explanation. Dachshunds, and dogs of similar body type, should never jump up onto and down from furniture any more than a book should fall from a shelf to the floor. Rose is always lifted up onto and down from the sofa. And just as we assist her, she helps us by arranging sofa pillows and afghans for maximum comfort.

Our eyes often cross, we cough, sneeze, wheeze, groan, or express ourselves in gross and unoriginal terms. We have identified a bibliose, a candidate for our stinky book treatment program.

The tea is for our throats, the tissues for our noses, and if the books are the banquet, the dachshund is the sorbet between courses. Between books we sniff our dog, our dear Rose Dackel, a natural sachet with her mild cinnamon scent. Dog sniffing clears our senses, calms our nerves, and is just plain fun. We also rub her tummy or give her a bit of a back rub.

We like books to smell like books—the paper and board and glue and leather equivalent of a clean, healthy dog fed well, groomed often, and loved constantly.

If your dog smelled unpleasant, you would inquire: Is it health, housing, diet, an encounter with a skunk? Books suffer from, and absorb the essences of, their environment, much as dogs and people do. Persistent dampness can make books smell unpleasant, as can smoking, cooking, or the decaying of a book's constituent properties. There seems to be a historical correlation between book collecting and smoking, especially pipes and cigars. It takes little imagination to see and smell what curls around the open book as the collector enjoys a good smoke and the warmth of a wood-burning fireplace. Some evidence of this little vision survives in books that smell bad or are stained with nicotine.

The goal is not just sensory. Eliminating odors, we've found, can reduce the potential for allergic reactions.

HOW TO MAKE AND USE A STINKY BOOK BOX

We use liquor cartons—they're sturdy, their dimensions allow room for most oversized books, and they're easy to replace. We also use plastic storage boxes, the kind sold in office supply stores.

Many other containers can be designated as stinky boxes: a covered plastic garbage pail, the drawer of a metal filing cabinet, a large suitcase or lined hamper. Receptacles need to be clean, dry, and without impartable odor, and must have dimensions appropriate to the books you need to treat. We once used a brand-new dishwasher as it sat over a long weekend, waiting to be installed. It did an excellent job, and we mention it only to suggest how full the world is of stinky box prospects. We would never use for book care a dishwasher that was hooked up to water or had ever washed a dish, but the appliance was ideal for one-time-only use. Keep in mind that your stinky box doesn't have to be a stinky box forever, and you'll never let an opportunity for fresh-smelling books slip away.

There's not much method involved: Select a clean carton or other container, add one or more solid room air fresheners, stand books upright inside, close tightly, and enjoy life while waiting for your books to recover. These commercial air fresheners come in a variety of scents. We've probably tried them all, and find that every fragrance works well.

Of course there are caveats: Take care that books remain upright in the stinky box. A book destunk is not improved by having bumped corners or creased pages. We often adjust the cardboard dividers in liquor cartons to accommodate books of various sizes while offering each one some stability. Some of the plastic storage boxes so widely available are equipped to hold hanging files; the rails in these boxes can help books stand securely while undergoing treatment.

Several products make useful destinkers. We started with shallow dishes of baking soda. Not bad, but messy and often requiring long destinking times. Our destinker of choice is now the solid room air freshener, the kind that comes in plastic cone-shaped containers. These do the job, and in a reasonable time; twenty-four hours are often sufficient, though we judge a book's readiness to return to society by our noses, never by the clock or calendar.

Also be careful that the destinker never touches your books.

The stinky book box itself will in time become stinky. Air it out if it won't sustain washing, with a sunbath if possible, or replace it if it's disposable, such as a liquor carton. Wash a plastic storage box or similar container with baking soda and water and, ideally, dry it in direct sunlight.

We often joke about developing a new kind of service dog. There are dogs who sniff for accelerants, cadavers, drugs, money, and explosives. We imagined a dog that would sniff books and identify those that needed destinking. We could save time and effort while giving our dogs, whose noses are far more discerning than ours, a new and important task.

Houdini sniffed a book for us once, discovered that it wasn't edible, and went back to bed. Rose, always eager for responsibility, sniffed several books, sneezed powerfully, and looked up at us with true pity, having learned the depths to which we descend to earn her kibble. So we sniff books ourselves, and Rose's sweet neck.

The stinky box as decorative object and gift: Decorate a liquor carton or other clean, closable receptacle, enclose a selection of air fresheners (unless you already know the recipient's taste for household aromas), and you have an interesting present. Add some old books to the box, and you have an even more interesting gift.

We think in terms of larger stinky boxes, capable of holding several books at a time. But there's no reason not to make a small decorative stinky box, just big enough for a single book. Made attractive, it might work as a book-end or book dummy, too.

Large or small, a stinky book box can be as beautiful as any decorative object. Ask the children to paint one for their grandparents, perhaps with scenes from summer vacation or images from the books the grandparents sent them for their last birthdays. Grandparents might decorate a stinky book box for their grandchildren—with scenes from old books that the younger generation may enjoy and care for one day; a nice older book might be enclosed or one of the crafts titles on making books or paper. The kids can use the box for treasures or toys as well as books.

Beyond Books

Some of the methods in this chapter clean so well that you may find, as we have, that they're useful throughout the home and office. For us, rubbing alcohol as a cleaner works wonders on metal or enamel doorknobs, kitchen and bathroom faucets and high-gloss cupboard finishes, metal window frames, mirrors, to name but a few of the things we clean when we cannot find a dirty book.

We use alcohol to remove fingerprints from the refrigerator door and spruce up small appliances, such as the food processor and the juicer; to keep bathroom tile free of soap scum and plastic wastebaskets spruce; to make oven doors and racks gleam; and, with cotton swabs, to tidy computer keyboards and fax and answering machines. For the sake of the dogs, we use rubbing alcohol on kitchen baseboards and flooring; morsels that escape from bowls and the place mats on which they sit ought not to be eaten off areas scrubbed with nasty chemicals. Another reason we clean with rubbing alcohol: It evaporates as it's used, and the smell it creates dissipates quickly.

The dry cleaning pad is a marvel of utility. Keep it handy for all arts-and-crafts projects. A spokesman for manufacturer Durosol Chemical also recommends its use on upholstery, lampshades, wallpaper, and clothing.

Try the stinky box for musty old letters, photographs, or anything paper that doesn't smell fresh.

(4)

REPAIRING

CAST an eye over any shelf of books, and you're bound to find one or two that are suitable for repair.

In addition to patience and the right products, for repair you will need some ingenuity and skill honed by practice. Before beginning, reread our mantras on pages 11–12. Most of all, remember that as the physician's oath is to "do no harm," the book repairer's is "do not make it worse." Never hesitate to do nothing.

Our emphasis is on common injuries that can be repaired by simple methods. In most cases, you will need only the basics: an adhesive and applicator, waxed paper, and pressure (exerted by the simplest forces, from rubber bands to heavy books serving as weights).

Before repairing a book, clean it. Cleaning reveals more about the book's condition. You also want to know the extent of damage before you embark on your repair. Book repair involves proximity, so a cleaner book means that your nose, hands, and eyes are exposed to fewer annoyances. When you finish the task, give the book a final cleaning to remove any fingerprints or residues that accumulated during repair.

Now and then you may have to choose between an aesthetic and a structural repair. Depending on what ails a book, you may decide that you care less about how the finished work looks and more about the book's stability. You may be willing to sacrifice looks for longevity when dealing with a book that is used constantly—a well-thumbed cookbook or bedside dictionary come to mind—but whose value is strictly utilitarian. Working on a fine binding, sentimental favorite, or well-established collectible entails another consideration: Alter the original as little as possible and avoid adding visible materials (except clear jackets).

Always keep in mind that this chapter is not a comprehensive survey of book injuries. Your books may have defects that require the skills of a professional bookbinder or restorer. Our advice: If your book's problem does not correspond to one described in this chapter, the book may need more than amateur care.

Glue: Remarks and a Dog Story

Glue is a wonderful invention, and a major tool in book first aid. We have always been glue fanatics, up at the crack of dawn to buy the newest, strongest, most exciting adhesive, rushing home to try it on whatever has obliged us by breaking, even carrying glue with us on social occasions, like a calling card, just in case.

When it comes to books, however, we are glue conservatives. Books need not the newest or most expensive glue, but the best glue for what books are made of: the transparent liquid plastics sold by archival supply houses and some stationers. And old-fashioned Elmer's.

Our many and varied glue experiences convince us that glue has a mind of its own and a tendency toward independent action. We may glue daily, yet glue still gets the better of us now and then. Glue can save the day, and restore the book, and it can make one hell of a mess. Practice glue control (keep the containers pristine, especially their applicator tops if you are proficient in their use, and properly sealed when not in use). Perfect the fine art of application (know not so much which is the best method of applying glue, but which method you do best, that gives you maximum control, with fine brushes, toothpicks, cotton swabs, or other implements). In describing specific tasks, we may refer to a particular applicator. When you perform the same task, use the method of glue application that is most efficient for you. Always have handy a rag for cleaning up the unexpected and for absorbing excess glue applied during repairs.

The good a little glue can do a book cannot be overstated. Use *a little* glue at a time, and lots of patience. Never hurry glue; it will set in its own time.

Glue sets best when you help it with pressure. You can weight a freshly glued book with another book, or make book weights by wrapping heavy flat objects in fabric or paper.

Not all glue tasks involve anything as elaborate as book weights. Some of the most spectacular improvements to an injured book can be attained by a drop of glue applied to a small paper or fabric flap or an endpaper corner peeling away from the inside of a front cover. After gluing, press the repaired area between your fingers. In many instances, that will be all the pressure you need.

Rubber bands can also exert uniform pressure. We often use four or five rubber bands, slipped horizontally over a closed book. We space the rubber bands over the height of the book, taking care to place one over any newly glued areas. If the covers are delicate, we may wrap the book in a clean cloth before adding the rubber bands. We favor flat, wide rubber bands; they are less likely to leave indentations in the covers and spine. Remove the rubber bands after several hours.

A single rubber band can be used in localized repairs, to hold a newly glued edge or part of a spine in place, but use the rubber band only long enough for the glue to set. Remember that rubber bands that are too tight and unattended can make lasting and ugly indentations in many bindings. Insert thin sheets of cardboard between a book and rubber bands to guard against wounding a book while the glue sets.

To some extent, glue is the high-wire act of simple amateur book repair. Don't glue without a net: proper ventilation and ample cleanup supplies. And no pets or kiddies underfoot when serious gluing is in progress. When it's time to glue, the book must have your undivided attention.

Of course, we have not always followed our own advice. During the years we had our shop, we often came in early, devoting the time before customers arrived to chores, like gluing, that can take up all your counter space and most of the floor.

Houdini, who still lives down the street from our old shop at a hotel where he supervises the front desk, always came in early, too.* A big, brawny dachshund—in build he resembles a wirehaired nuclear submarine—Houdini has more than the usual dog's knack for making himself comfortable. Toss a coat on the sofa, and Houdini would add it to the blankets on his bed. Leave a handbag on the floor, and Houdini would turn it into a pillow. Glue a book, leave it on the floor for a moment because the telephone rang, and when you returned, you'd discover Houdini on top of the book and sound asleep. With the keen instincts of a bookselling professional, he always—there were numerous instances—positioned his massive chest on top of the book and flopped, inelegantly but adorably. We could do nothing but drape a shawl over his shoulders.

---

*Rose rarely worked in the shop. She put in long hours in the office and did a great deal of work at home. She knew about the mice in the shop's woodwork, and was determined to dig them out. While she was happy to meet people, she took a dim view of many retail norms. We thought it was perfectly fine to make people welcome, to encourage them to take any book off the shelves, poke around, and browse to their hearts' content. Rose barked if a customer touched anything. If we handed books to a customer, Rose was tolerant, but made it clear that she considered the whole escapade unwise at best. And there was no getting out the door with purchases. A kind soul once stopped, stooped down, and showed Rose a receipt. It did no good: Rose sniffed the receipt, but still grasped the shopping bag of books in her teeth and dragged it back to us. She never developed into the great sales dog that Houdini became. In business, her strength remains in back-office decision-making.

We don't recommend that dogs moonlight as book weights, but when they do, check that the dog's weight is evenly distributed over the book. But only if in so doing, you do not disturb the dog.

A Recipe: Our Favorite Paste

❧

With so many adhesives on the market, why bother to make your own? It may be nostalgia: Perhaps you made paste in a kindergarten arts and crafts class. Perhaps you're a do-it-yourselfer who reasons that if you're going to repair your own books you ought to use your own paste. Maybe it's the middle of the night when you run out of Elmer's.

There are probably as many variations on homemade paste as there are for chicken soup. Flour, cornmeal, and gluten-free wheat starch all have their champions. Following is the recipe that has worked best for us.

In a double boiler over medium-high heat, mix 2 tablespoons of white flour with 2 tablespoons of water.

Stir gently as the mixture warms.

Add another 8 tablespoons of water. Mix well.

Cook for about 5 minutes, stirring to prevent lumps from forming. The paste is ready when it's thick and opalescent, moving against your spoon or spatula like a gummy buttercream frosting. Remove it from the stove and let the brew cool.

Apply the paste when it has reached room temperature. Store in a covered container, but not for long. (Consider a receptacle that is not associated with food. We know of pasters who have spread their homemade product on toast, just because it was stored in an old marmalade jar!) It won't keep longer than a few days, and turns rubbery and strange after a week or so even when refrigerated. Discard it at the first sign of mold.

This version works best in small doses on lightweight paper, in both book repair and art projects. Use too much, and you risk soaking into and buckling paper. It can be applied with the usual implements, from brushes to toothpicks. Or use your fingertips, a precision method that's not appealing with other adhesives—and one that may bring back happy memories of fingerpainting.

A cleanup hint: Chill a pot to which more than a glaze of paste clings. Most of the remaining paste will then lift off easily or peel away with a spatula. Routine cleanup calls for no more than warm, soapy water. Paste residue dissolves under running water, and should not cause drain or septic tank disorders.

More reasons to make your own paste: A homemade product may be appropriate for children's use. It's safer to play with a flour-and-water adhesive than with a chemical product. It's easy to clean up—off the floor, little hands, and smocks.

Homemade paste also makes an unusual gift, suitable for all occasions. Present it in some lovely little piece of crockery, with a handmade label and a flourish or two—perhaps a single rose or some sweets.

The Dust Jacket
❦

Tears (especially along the folds), chips, and holes afflict paper dust jackets. Most tears can be closed. Remove the jacket from the book, place it face down—making sure that the torn areas are properly positioned—and affix invisible tape on the inner side. Take care that tape does not extend beyond the jacket's edges.

Chips (missing portions of a jacket's edges) and holes can often be repaired if the absent portions are at hand. More often than not, the missing pieces are just that, and all you can do is reinforce surrounding areas and hope that chips and holes are not enlarged.

In a pinch, patch: Fill in a hole or compensate for a chip with plain paper (or something jazzy if the spirit moves you). Using invisible tape, affix patches on the inside of the jacket. This is a last resort, however, appropriate only when the stability of the dust jacket is at risk and when clear protective covers are not available.

A chipped, torn, or hole-ridden dust jacket is always best preserved with a protective cover (see pages 101–5).

The External Book
❦

You may have reupholstered an armchair after removing its several layers and discovering how it was made, or reconstructed a cabinet that fell apart by treating it like a puzzle. You may be delighted with lasting good results, or chagrined that you did the work yourself.

To examine many of the injuries common to the external book is to face a similar quandary. What ails the book seems obvious. All its parts are present, apparently, so you should be able to put it back together again: the case (covers and spine) and the hinges (by which the text block and case are joined by endpapers).

Keep in mind, however, that sometimes putting it back together is not the same as effecting a genuine repair or restoration. We'll point out the distinctions as we go along, in the hope of helping you decide what you can do, when you should do nothing, and when only a professional can help.

⟿

LOOSE AND BROKEN HINGES Open a book. Does the front or back cover wobble? If so, chances are that the book has a loose hinge. You may see endpapers or the text block pulling away from the inside of the case, with the spine lining visible and intact. This sounds like a broken hinge. In other words, the book is in one piece, but it is separating. It needs prompt attention because the stability of the book is at risk.

If the endpapers are loose at the hinge and no longer firmly and continuously attached to the inside of the cover, or the text block, or both, they must be reattached. Examine the book, with the cover open, by looking at it from top and bottom. You should be able to see the separation, like a chute extending from one edge of the cover or flyleaf. Coat a slender knitting needle, skewer, or chopstick with glue. Insert the applicator under the separated endpaper.

Taking care not to puncture the endpaper, urge glue as far inside the separation as possible. Rotate the applicator to distribute the glue. When you withdraw the knitting needle or other applicator, watch for excess glue emerging from the work area. Tidy up any excess glue promptly with a rag. Run a bone folder over the tightened hinge or text block. Close the book and weight it overnight.

More-serious damage can also be repaired simply. On opening a book, you may notice a gap between the inside of a cover and the text block; the cover and text block remain attached but a chasm is growing between them where the endpapers have parted. Assuming that the spine and its interior parts are intact, you can proceed as follows. Lay a piece of waxed paper along the text block and another on the inside of the open cover. The waxed paper sheets should leave only the gap exposed. Carefully apply adhesive to the exposed area. Be sure that the case and text block are properly aligned. Wipe away any excess glue immediately. Leave the waxed paper in place when you close the book. Secure the book with rubber bands and weight it overnight.

Single- or double-stitched binder tapes manufactured for hinge repair or any cloth tape can also be used if you are not concerned about appearance.

These instructions cover only the hinge injuries that can be fixed easily. Tackle more-complicated hinge problems only after you have mastered our advice and are keen for more-advanced work. Never neglect loose or broken hinges. A hinge is just as important to a book as it is to your front door.

❧

SPINES The spine is more than what you see when a book is shelved. Spines may be beautifully decorated or gilt-stamped, but plain or fancy, the more books you have, the more their spines are part of your decor and overall environment. That is just one reason why spines should always look their best. Another reason is that the backbone of a book takes stress much like the spine of a human does, though a book's resultant woes can be more readily fixed. We often wonder if books would last longer and be less prone to injuries if they were made more like dogs, who have the good spine sense to walk on all fours.

Sometimes a spine detaches, peeling away from the head or tail, or opening "like a book" from the front or back cover. If the covers and hinges are secure, then glue and pressure are all you need to give the spine first aid.

Examine the spine's lining or backing. Does it appear to be in relatively good shape? Are there any obvious missing pieces or wear? Check for any weakening of attachments to the text block. Depending on the book's age and construction, you may find old newspaper or other potential artifacts lining the spine. Detailed work, including replacement of the inner portions of a spine, are beyond novice book repair.

When a portion of an old spine is missing, revealing the bound end of the text block, you may want to protect the book with clear polyester film. If the exposed text block is coming apart, you may want to reinforce it with cloth tape.

❧

FRAYING Corners, the edges of covers, and spines often fray or suffer abrasions, especially when bound in fabric. When upholstery or clothing frays, a stitch or two usually do the trick. For books, adhesive is the answer.

A freshly glued spine should be secured with rubber bands. Guard against indentations caused by the rubber bands; strips of cardboard between the rubber bands and the spine do the trick. Corners and edges surrounded by waxed paper can be weighted with books while glue sets.

Library suppliers sell die-cut "corners" to repair and reinforce those parts of a book that are badly frayed. These cloth, or clothlike, items are self-adhesive, with a peel-away backing. The same suppliers usually market self-adhesive reinforcers, known as "wings," to repair and protect the heads and tails of badly worn spines. These are good products, and not difficult to use, but remember that their effects are not discreet. Before using them, decide how much you are willing to alter a book's appearance.

❧

DETACHED COVERS If a book is rare or valuable, bound in leather, or simply a very good book, a detached cover should be restored only by a professional. The work may be expensive, but it may be a good investment.

For a book that you would discard rather than invest in, there are do-it-yourself alternatives. These alternatives are not orthodox book repair, but measures taken in extremis. Think twice before following our instructions: Are you salvaging something like an old car repair manual, just to keep it going, or are you dealing with a book that you might someday treat to a visit to the bookbinder? If you might splurge one of these days, do nothing to the book but keep it safe.

If you decide to do it yourself, you might try it with a companion. One of you will be responsible for positioning, the other for rejoining the book's parts.

To reattach a cover, place the book flat. Position the detached cover as if it were undamaged, the book lying open. Run the tape of your choice along the re-created hinge.

If a book's spine needs first aid and a cover reattached as well, repair the spine first.

There are a host of specialty tapes manufactured for use in book repair, including adhesive-backed cloth tapes in colors that are especially appropriate for use on spines. Binder tapes designed to rejoin covers are also available, with such features as a built-in flexible hinge, resistance to tears and mildew, and permanent adhesives.

There are no civil or criminal penalties for using duct tape; it's strong and flexible. You can use adhesive tape for the same properties. Your sense of book decency will prevent your using either product. No repair is so urgent that it cannot wait until you have a tape more appropriate for use on books.

☙

DETACHED CASE This is not work for the amateur. When a good book loses its covers and spine, it needs professional care.

We mention this injury because it's sometimes deceptive. It may look simple to repair—the case (spine and covers) is in one piece, which is itself in good repair, and the text block is separate but sound. You may be tempted to fix it yourself. But this is one temptation we urge you to resist. Why? The repair may work at first. But it is unlikely to last, especially if the book is often opened, its pages turned. You will be disappointed. The book will be in sorrier shape than it was before you mended it. Being put back together is, in this case, not the same as being made whole.

The stumbling block is stitching. Older books were commonly stitched. A detached case often means that stitching, the sewing by hand or machine of the signatures that make up the text block, is exposed. Stitching and glue do not mix. Stitching and glue must not meet.

However, are you dealing with a book in which there is no stitching or whose stitching is not exposed? Does it meet your risk-versus-value criteria? Do you need to refer to the book, but know you won't unless it's reassembled?

Working on a modern book without exposed stitching, you might consider the following method to fix a cleanly detached case—*if the case (spine and covers) is in one piece, which is itself in good repair, and the text block is separate but sound.* When you examine the two parts of the book, you may see tracks from the original adhesive; you may follow these with your application of glue, but don't stint.

Before gluing, however, you may want to scrape off any dried glue or other matter that might impede perfect matching of the case and the text block.

Apply glue to both the inside of the spine and the bound end of the text block. Waxed paper can be used to protect against glue overflow where the spine and text block meet. Close the book, protect it with cardboard sheets, and slip rubber bands over the cardboard, spacing them nicely. They should be snug enough to exert ample pressure on the spine. Let the book rest overnight.

This method works well with the odd paperback book whose spine peels away, taking the covers with it.

The Internal Book
ᛉ

The most common injuries to the contents of a book, the text block, lend themselves to simple do-it-yourself repairs.

ᛉ

PAPER TEARS There are ways of closing (mending) tears with rice paper and other exotic materials that are extolled in standard book repair manuals. We've had little luck, and a few mishaps, with these professional-style methods. Similarly, we don't favor tape; even invisible tape cut to the dimensions of a tear will be an eyesore.

We've had great success with a method simpler than most taught for this purpose, and one that gives a better result than taping does.

1. Rest the torn page on a sheet of waxed paper.
2. Run a line of glue, using a fine paintbrush, along the tear.
3. Wipe away any excess glue—glue that extends beyond the immediate area of the tear—with a cloth or cotton swab.
4. Place a second sheet of waxed paper on top of the torn page.

5. Close the book, for a tear-in-a-waxed-paper sandwich, and squeeze it for a minute or two.

6. Rest the book flat on its cover and place atop it a heavy object, such as a book weight or another book or two. The extra weight forces the glue into the edges of the tear. Let the book sit overnight. Most glues that are appropriate to use on book paper take time to set.

7. Later, on opening the book to the torn page, remove the two sheets of waxed paper. There may be a modest scar where the tear was, but the tear is now securely closed.

This method may have an aesthetic drawback, but it is an easy way to prevent a tear from worsening and causing lasting damage to a book.

❧

LOOSE PAGES By "loose" we mean that a page—title, text page, or full-page illustration—is no longer attached to the book. It can become damaged or lost if not reattached. It should never be used as a bookmark.

There are several ways to reattach loose pages. You can carefully position the page, making sure that it lines up evenly at its three edges, and run lengths of invisible tape along the gutter, turning the page and repeating the process, thus creating a tape hinge for the page. You can also mix a highball of vodka and vinegar. We recommend neither.

Here is how we prefer to do it, once again turning to that great trio—glue, waxed paper, and pressure: Open the book to the appropriate place and run the thinnest possible line of glue along the gutter with a fine paintbrush or a flat toothpick. Insert the loose page with a dabbing wiggle and a nudge to encourage the glue and paper to meet. Then insert sheets of waxed paper on either side of the reattached page; the sheets should reach into the gutter to keep glue from adhering to any paper except that of the page on which you are working. Close the book and slip wide rubber bands around it horizontally. Rubber bands exert pressure toward the spine, helping the reinserted page take root. Leave the rubber bands in place for several hours.

If the gutter side of the loose page is ragged, you can trim the most pronounced projections before reattachment. If the page is torn, repair it (see pages 69–70) before restoring it to the book.

A loose signature (a unit of book pages) can usually be restored as if it were a single leaf.

Sometimes you will find in the text block a separation that resembles a loose hinge. Depending on the book's construction, you may notice a crack in the spine, or the spine may look fine and function normally while only the text block has weakened. A book may fall open to a particular place. Or on turning pages you may observe stitching or other components deep in the book's gutter.

If you suspect that the text block needs stabilizing, leaf through the book, looking for the area or areas of worst separation. Lay the book open to the damaged area. Place lengths of waxed paper on both pages. Position each one deep in the gutter. The waxed paper lengths should not meet. Allow between them only space enough to run a fine brush. With the brush, apply adhesive as deep as you can into the gutter. Remove any excess. Then close the book, with the waxed paper sheets inside, and weight it for several hours. The goal in this repair is to force the book's pages to adhere not only to each other but to the spine's lining. So this is one of the classic cases in which wide rubber bands are ideal.

A loose-page caveat: If the book was originally sewn, loose pages or signatures should be restored by sewing. To use glue is to risk damage caused by the seepage of glue into the paper and thread.

DOG-EARS Dogs, bless them, have all sorts of ears: pricked ears that remind us of Strongheart and Rin-Tin-Tin; semierect ears like Lassie's; pendant ears like those of our beloved dachshunds; and a score of evocative sub-types, including tulip, rose, button, bat, and bear ears, to name but a few.

Books have dog-ears of one regrettable type, the turned-down corner. People do it to mark the page to which they want to return. No doubt they do so only because they lack the book-friendly flat place-keeping device or the ability to remember where they left off.

A creased corner is not a major problem, nor is the occasional creased page. It can be an eyesore, but it can be fun to fix.

We first tried to fix a dog-ear after watching an old English movie. The very proper butler carried the *Times* into the pantry. He ironed it before presenting it, on a sil-ver tray, to his employer.

Set your iron on its lowest temperature, and dry heat only—no steam! Slip a dry, clean cloth or sheets of waxed paper below and above the dog-eared page, and press the warm iron on the dog-ear. Not every crease will be eradicated by this method, but most will be greatly reduced and the dog-ear will evolve from pendant to pricked-ear stance.

In extreme cases, the crease caused by a dog-ear can weaken the paper until the dog-ear falls off. You must decide which you prefer: a page corner absent or a page corner reinforced with invisible tape.

You can also treat an amputated dog-ear as you would any paper tear. Place a sheet of waxed paper under the affected page, apply glue along the page edge, position the dog-ear so that it gathers glue and sits in its original spot. Place another sheet of waxed paper on top, close the book, and rest it for several hours under a book weight or a couple of heavy books. When you remove the waxed paper sheets, you will doubtless see where the dog-ear is rejoined to the page.

Homemade Book Weights

When weighting books, two considerations are important. First, weight should be distributed evenly. Second, avoid placing weights directly on the spine of the book being weighted.

Books themselves make good weights. As a general rule, select for a weight a book larger than the one being weighted. If the book used as a weight is not particularly heavy, add more books (size is now less important) on top of it, or other flat objects.

Dedicated book weights: Using books as weights is just the beginning. You can make formal book weights with items you probably have around the house. Wrapping paper or fabric taped around a brick or stout piece of lumber is just the start.

Family and friends may welcome book weights as an unexpected gift. With personalized decorations, perhaps reflecting the recipient's taste in literature, these could be the ultimate surprise for someone who has everything. Made solid and attractive, a good book weight can double as a doorstop. Depending on its dimensions and covering, it might also serve as a book dummy, to keep books vertical when shelves are not full, or as a bookend.

When a Book Gets Wet

Treatment of a wet book cancels the rule on patience. Act instantly! If you reach a book the moment the garden sprinklers splatter it, or retrieve it from the bathtub just as it hits the water, you have a chance to minimize damage. But let water dry and stain book paper, and you have a problem beyond the scope of amateur book care.

If the book has a dust jacket, remove it. Quickly but gently pat dry the dust jacket (both sides), the book's covers and spine, and all book pages. Use dry sponges, clean bath towels, or any other absorbent cloth that's handy, including your clothing. Single-ply paper towels absorb moisture, but they may disintegrate, adding shreds of wet toweling to dry on damp book surfaces. A double-ply paper towel will not only absorb more moisture; it is less likely to leave debris that you will have to remove from the book.

A hair dryer, at its lowest temperature, can help propel the water away from paper surfaces and spines. A lot depends on the paper. Coated paper and dust jackets will soak up water more slowly than uncoated paper.

When you have removed as much excess water as possible by blotting, carefully open the book, inserting sheets of double-ply paper towel, such as Bounty, between covers and endpapers. Then carefully part the pages, inserting paper towel between the pages. This keeps the pages from clinging together, and allows for some evaporation. Replace each sheet of paper towel as often as necessary, which will be frequently. No double-ply paper towels handy? Start the process with waxed paper, which will keep pages from adhering one to the other, and try to stand the book upright so that its pages are not compressed; waxed paper can allow moisture to evaporate back into book paper. Replace the waxed paper with double-ply paper towels as quickly as you can.

You can use a variant of the stinky book box to help wet books recuperate. You'll need a damp-resistant container and an absorbent natural product, such as pipe tobacco. Sprinkle stale pipe tobacco in the container, and place the book inside, double-ply paper towels still between the pages. Periodically check the book for progress. Replace the double-ply paper towel sheets as they gather moisture.

Another aid is one you probably have handy, unless you live at either pole and it's winter. Joe Landau of FineBinding.com offered the following emergency advice for a book that has been wet and thoroughly blotted: sunlight. "It dries it in a slow, uniform way," Joe said, recommending natural sunlight (no sunlamps, please), "in a warm spot that isn't too humid." You might place the book in a window for three hours a day, during the middle of the day. If there are covers that might fade in the sun, shield them from the light, letting them absorb the warmth. Joe pointed out that while this is the only excuse for exposing a book to sunlight, there is good reason to try it in such an extreme case. "It accomplishes two things," he said. The method dries books without baking them, and it retards the growth of spores and bacteria, which books might acquire in the bathwater or punchbowl or, when wet, from the surrounding air. "There are always spores in the air, and spores are activated by temperature and humidity," Joe pointed out, adding that ultraviolet light will kill most spores.

What Can't Be Helped

Certain injuries do not lend themselves to easy repair. Among the problems you are more likely to encounter are bumped corners (you might massage them between your fingers; some corners will improve this way and take on some of their original shape if not much crispness or resilience), warped covers and rolled spines (most do-it-yourself efforts do more harm than good), and peeling (when layers on some modern dust jackets separate, the sure remedy is a clear protective jacket; when laminate boards peel, cut clear polyester film from a roll to fit snugly). Except for conditions amenable to a drop of glue, manufacturing defects defy amateur repairs.

A Visit with a Bookbinder
❦

It's time to introduce you to one of the professionals whose care we have recommended you seek when a book requires it. We'll also try to give you some idea of what a book craftsperson can do for you and your collection, what you might expect to pay for a few of the most common repairs and restorations, and some insights into routine book maintenance from someone who has seen it all. Before we could say "bibliopegist," we were off to see our friend the bookbinder.

Joseph Landau's company, FineBinding.com, operates in corner offices on the second floor above busy Madison Avenue in what his Web site (www.finebinding.com) identifies as "the heart of the art and photography district." Sitting with Joe, we were still in midtown Manhattan, the Empire State Building a near neighbor, uptown buses rushing past but muted by a reassuring environment: books elaborate and simple everywhere at hand, the aroma of good paper and leather, and, from the far end of the room, the sounds of a craftsman restoring a splendid old book. He was using tools that a bookbinder of centuries ago would recognize. What he did to that book a bookbinder of centuries ago would have done the same way.

The hand-binding of books may seem a bit arcane these days, when most of us buy our books bound. Not too many generations back, however, book buyers would have expected to make choices about a binding the way we do about the upholstery in a new car. What we encountered at Joe's office was a place where old and new meet and prosper. Books are as contemporary as today's news, yet at the bookbinder's you can watch them made and mended the original way, no electricity or other "improvements" required.

Joe's career in books goes back to the early 1980s, when he managed the Brentano's Fifth Avenue store. "We had an old and rare book section there, and that was one of my responsibilities." Brentano's bought as well as sold old books and offered customers a book repair service. "We didn't do it there, in house, but we sent it out to different binders, and I became interested in it. I began to learn on my own." Joe already owned the Jamaica Book Center, in Queens, New York, which had the distinction of opening "in the year Babe Ruth hit sixty home runs" (1927), said Joe. The Queens store, which closed in 1992, sold old, rare, and used books, and like Brentano's, bought books from customers and put customers in touch with bookbinders.

⚜

FINDING A BOOKBINDER When you decide you need a bookbinder, how can you find one? "Know any bookbinders?" drew blank stares from the people we asked during one of our explorations of what we assumed was common knowledge to everyone but us. We asked thoughtful, well-informed folk known for loving books, dusting them now and then, and even trying to keep the sun from shining on their spines, or just their books' spines. These are the sort of friends and acquaintances who can be counted on for the best in baby-sitters and plumbers, hairdressers and dog walkers, gurus in every legal and medical specialty; one was prepared to give us the name of a reliable taxidermist. But no one knew a bookbinder. Many said they would have asked us for such a referral, if we hadn't asked them first. Most suggested we consult the *Yellow Pages*.

Now, we asked Joe how the public can find a bookbinder, and how his customers find him. He, too, suggested the *Yellow Pages,* calling it "probably the most democratic way a person can go about finding a bookbinder." There are professional associations, he acknowledged, but their referrals may favor their members, and a fine craftsperson may just not be the joining kind. How do his customers find him? At present, he said, "It's about 50 percent word of mouth, 30 percent Internet, 20 percent *Yellow Pages,* but it changes all the time."

How can a book lover choose the right bookbinder from among prospects? "I think if you go to somebody who's a bookbinder, you should get a recommendation from somebody else—we provide that for our customers. We keep a stack of references."

Customers who visit his office always ask to see references, and samples of materials, he said. "That's 100 percent of the time." And, of course, examples of work that are comparable to the work they need done.

For customers who come calling via the Internet, service is just as complete. "What I've done over the last year is to build a database. I take photographs of everything that we do. We put it on the computer, and when people contact us over the Internet, and they ask us for something specific, there's that specific something to show them. Just about every reply goes out with a photograph of what, essentially, it is they want. So they always see for themselves. I try to make it simple." When customers want to see samples of material, they can receive—by conventional means—swatches of linen or leather or whatever is contemplated for the work under discussion.

❧

REPAIRS AND PRICES We talked about the kind of repairs and restorations the average book lover and collector most often needs. Joe said that what he sees most often is a book that is falling apart. "First thing we look at are the pages—are the pages loose? If the pages are loose, they need to be resewn. And what you want to do ideally is to resew it in the fashion that it was sewn originally. Most old books were sewn in signature, and so they have to be sewn through the middles of the signatures and then the signatures need to be attached."

Depending on a book's condition and the acidity and brittleness of its components, the repair can get more complicated. Joe noted that some old books' parchment or paper may be acid-free, not by design as they would be today, but by good fortune. Then there are books much harder to repair. "Often, if a book was originally sewn in signature, you can't resew it in signature only because the book paper is so brittle that you can't go through the signatures. You have to sew it from the top, which is called oversewing, and that's a machine process. That you don't want to do, but if the book's falling apart and the only way to put it back together would be to sew it from the top, then you have to tell the customer that; how you're going to go about sewing it; what you recommend. You may have to make the decision, but ideally the paper is good enough so that you can hand-sew it through the signatures, [and then] attach the signatures." To machine-sew a book of six by nine inches, Joe said, costs about $60. Done by hand, the sewing "would cost probably about $150, because it takes two or three hours. Some books, it takes days to do."

Then the resewn book must be reunited with its boards. "To hand-sew a book and recover it in a linen cover or the original cover?" Joe calculated. "It may be as much as $225 or $250."

In pricing, Joe explained, each job is broken down into individual tasks. "You have to estimate the time. It's not the materials, even in a leather book. Let's say a leather skin for a book costs about $60. That's only part, that's your basic material costs, aside from paper and thread, which is minimal. Your real cost, 80 percent of your cost, is labor, time."

A restoration such as reattaching a board might cost $150, Joe reported, and the process is expensive for good reason: the extensive labor that precedes the reattachment. What's involved? Pulling back linen or leather, sanding the attaching edge so that, when the restoration is complete, the board will meet the spine with precision.

Joe mentioned damage to endpapers as another problem he sees frequently. "If you replace the endpapers, both endpapers? Let's say a book fell from a shelf, and that's very common, and the rest of the book is okay, but both endpapers are torn or the book is separated from the endpapers. That's a couple hours' work, so it's about a $50 or $60 repair, depending on the size of the book."

Joe spoke at length about the merits of authenticity, authenticity's effect on the value of books, and the need for book lovers to factor these into their decisions. Asked if he ever tells customers not to proceed with a certain project—adding a new cover to an old book, for example—he didn't hesitate: "All the time," he said. "If they have a valuable book and they're concerned it doesn't look that good to them"—Joe stopped to reach for a book of the Civil War era, whose owner had at first wanted to have the cover replaced. "Look how lousy it looks. That's actually a repaired book. But the thing is, it's repaired in such a way that it retains more of its value in this state than if it had a new cover."

Both bookbinder and book owner need to understand each other's perspectives when planning any major work on an old volume. "You have to explain to [customers] . . . that this kind of repair, where you're restoring as much of the original as possible, costs more than actually putting a new cover on. *That* you have to let them know off the bat. And I usually let them know that from the ease of work, it's much easier to put on a new cover, much harder to restore it. It takes a lot less time to recover a book than it does to restore a book. But if they're interested in authenticity, if they're interested in value, if it's a rare book, they should have the book restored as opposed to having a new cover. But if it's for their own reading purposes, if it's something they're going to use all the time, I'd rather have a nice cover on a book than a restored cover. Just depends on what the need is, what the value is—there are a lot of things involved." Above all, Joe emphasized, he wants to know "what the goals of the customer are."

"ARCHIVAL" We asked Joe about the term *archival* in his work. The term is used so often to describe products, including many that we use all the time on our merchandise and that the suppliers we recommend for home book care and repair use to denote a certain kind of quality and appropriateness for particular uses. We wondered if in the world of bookbinding, "archival" was becoming what "organic" has become in the supermarket and elsewhere. "Archival only means that you're using materials that are going to, from what you understand, last and keep the book alive for a long period of time. That doesn't mean that you can't use certain processes that are quick and inexpensive and not be archival at the same time. I'm always suspicious of the term *archival*. The word *archival* is new, and we don't know how long an archivally repaired or rebound book is going to last. I mean, the jury is going to be in, in about a hundred years."

STAINS Another thing the jury may still be out on is the best way to treat stains on book paper. We have often been tempted by the cleaning potions touted in catalogs, and have had mixed results with them. Are we using the products incorrectly, despite following the instructions, or have we not had precisely the right stains on the right kinds of paper for the products we've tried?

Joe was emphatic. "Removing stains from paper is the hardest thing to do. And we don't normally do it." It's "quite expensive," he said. He knows of no one unfailing product or method for removing stains from book paper—"we have all sorts of things that we use"—but keeps on hand a selection of old books that are valuable only for the variety of different papers they contain. Before working on a stain, Joe explained, he matches the stained book paper with paper from his store of expendables, and tests until he finds the right method and product for the task. He often refers customers to specialists who restore documents. The Internet is one place to find these magicians. Dealers in autograph letters and other paper ephemera may also be able to help.

※

CUSTOMIZED ITEMS You can ask bookbinders for more than repairs and restorations. Joe Landau's business makes customized bookplates, slipcases, clamshell boxes, portfolios, and personalized albums, diaries, and sketchbooks. In short, if what you want is in any way booklike or related to books, a bookbinder can probably produce, repair, and restore it for you.

Joe has a special affinity for graphic design. It was during his tenure at Brentano's, where his responsibilities included the store's art and prints department, that he mastered the processes—lithography, engraving, and the like—and began to develop into the artist he is today. He showed us a die he had just produced. "This design is for a yearbook that has fallen apart, and this all has to be graphically done before the metal plates are made. What I'm personally best known for is my graphic work. That's why a lot of corporations come to me, because, I feel, that with the [computer] programs that I use and my experience, I can design just about any kind of graphic for a book. And for corporations, that's very important."

For individuals, personalized albums are much in demand: photo albums and albums to commemorate weddings and other events. Existing books can also be personalized and decorated for special occasions, as we learned when we asked for another example of a recent original work. "I just finished a dictionary for a bar mitzvah for a young man, and I designed a menorah for the cover of the book. That menorah took a week to do. Because, when I do it, I usually make variations on a theme. So I don't just say to the customer, 'Here it is, this is what I've designed for you.' I say, 'Here are the choices.' He chose one design, and we made a plate from it, and we stamped it on the book. It was an original design, so that nobody says, 'Oh, I saw that menorah in *Better Homes and Gardens.*' No, it's a menorah that came from FineBinding.com." The price for a future heirloom like this? Between $700 and $800.

In addition to one-of-a-kind pieces for individuals, Joe also serves a range of corporate clients—from Merrill Lynch to Chase Bank to New York Life—and makes all sorts of props for the entertainment industry. HBO, Disney, and Miramax have been among his clients, along with the directors Ron Howard and Martin Scorsese and Broadway's *Beauty and the Beast*. "Movie companies want scripts," he said. "Film companies want props. They want boxes made. They want books to look a certain way."

❧

BOOK MAINTENANCE Probably every book owner wants books to look a certain way, even when the stage is just the living room wall or the cabinets in the study. Maintaining that "certain way" depends to a great degree on how books are kept and handled.

"Take care of them" is Joe's admonition to the owners of books. First and foremost, he said, is knowing how to handle a book. "So many people will destroy or harm their book in the first hour of owning it. They'll put it on the shelf and then want to look at it—they'll put their finger on top and rip the dust jacket. Years ago, the dust jacket meant nothing in people's minds, but now the dust jacket of a first edition is actually worth a lot more than the book itself."

Joe said that serious collectors understand the importance of dust jackets, but the novice and the average book buyer may not be giving it much thought. "They'll still bring in books in perfect condition with ratty covers. So, you know, I'm of two minds with that. Because the dust jacket is really designed or made to protect the book, but it seems things are reversed. You need to protect the dust jacket too, if you want to maintain the value, especially of a fiction book or book of poetry. Especially those two categories. The jacket design is worth something."

In the same vein, Joe reasoned that while books are "pretty resilient," and don't need to be kept in sterile environments, they do need us to treat them with common sense. The kind of care that comes from common sense may be almost too obvious. Joe wondered if one of the reasons so many books fall apart is that they're so easy to take care of that people don't think about it.

We asked Joe to share his thoughts about it, for more guidance on the environmental factors and housekeeping principles that make books live longer.

Sunlight: "You want to keep your books, if they're not wet, out of the sunlight. Because sunlight is a bleacher. It bleaches materials—whether it's leather, whether it's linen, whether it's paper—it bleaches it. So prolonged exposure to sunlight is harmful to books."

Temperature and humidity: Joe said that sixty degrees and 60 percent, respectively, were ideal for books, but admitted that "that's impractical in terms of living. For example, if you go to the Museum of Modern Art and you go down to their photography vault downstairs, where they keep all the stuff you don't see on the walls, you have to wear a sweater or a coat down there. It's cold. And it's that way for a reason." Is there a sensible compromise? Joe's recommendation is that a home's temperature not exceed seventy degrees, with humidity maintained at no more than 70 percent.

Dust and the acid test: The air we breathe, and that surrounds our books, has acid content, Joe pointed out. "The combination of dust and humidity creates a very acid environment, especially here in New York," adding that the pH of its air might put the city on the same plane as some lakes. "If you get dust on books, and you don't wipe it off, that dust will begin to deteriorate the paper and then you're inviting spores, also mold, mildew." Joe suggested keeping books behind glass to protect them against airborne hazards. If a glass-enclosed library is beyond your budget or otherwise unappealing, create a mini environment behind glass for your most precious books. We once saw half a dozen fine bindings between dolphin-shaped bookends. A fish tank sat, upside down, like a dome over the entire display. When books are stored behind glass, they need periodic airing.

Shelving: The shelving is metal at FineBinding.com. Though he agreed that it may not be appealing for home bookshelves, Joe prefers metal; it's safe for books and it's serviceable. "It's easier to keep clean," he said. Wood, on the other hand, is an organic substance that can stain and hold moisture; "It's more dangerous to the book."

Caring for leather bindings: For years we have used a well-known leather dressing for bindings, and have been pleased with the results. Just before our meeting with Joe, we learned that the Northeast Document Conservation Center, esteemed in its field, warned against the use of leather dressings. NEDCC worried that the dressings could cause problems, including ". . . stickiness of the leather, wicking of oil into adjoining materials, including text blocks, and increased danger of mold growth on treated materials." We wondered if, as the NEDCC statement alluded, one of the problems with leather dressing is that it's so easy to use too much. It's gratifying to use leather dressing—it's rich stuff, and to work with it is not unlike playing with food (anyone remember making mashed potato dams, with extra butter, by hand?). It's a product that must be applied sparingly—to the point of self-denial. We asked Joe for his opinion. He uses the same product we use (from Talas). "We're very happy with it," he said, adding that "it all comes down to chemistry and how the leather dressing reacts with the leather." He theorized that different leathers—calfskin, pigskin, goatskin—may react differently, but can be treated with leather dressing, and caution.

A worthwhile task: "You should rotate your books on your shelf." Joe imagined an average household, with a wooden bookcase of four wide shelves. On each shelf, 30 to 40 volumes, for a total of perhaps 150 books. "And those books often don't even get touched for years. There is moisture accumulation. Some books are tightly bound. Some books are loosely bound. There's moisture accumulation in your books." Joe's advice continued: "You should take your books off the shelf, flip through your books, air them out, close them up, put them back on the shelf, and rotate them so that if one book happens to have a mold growth, it doesn't infect the other books." Any book with a sign of mold, of course, comes off the shelf. Immediately.

A household early warning system: "I find once in a while that when there's been a leak in the roof, you may first discover it in your bookshelves," Joe told us. Water seems to be drawn to books. It flows naturally around the edges of shelves, seeping under and into books. It can flow into absorbent books without the dripping—visible or audible—that might otherwise alert you to a leak. "I had a first edition of a Joseph Heller book, *Something Happened,* which is a very nice book," Joe said. "And it was ruined because there was a leak in my roof, a very insidious tiny leak that had just found its way to that book." So it makes sense to rotate books on shelves, looking for signs of trouble. Look at the books, look behind the books now and then, run your hand along the back of a shelf where it may be easier to feel wet than see it. Catch a bookshelf leak early, and you may have only minor damage to your library. And you may spare more than your books. Your entire home and all your possessions and your pocketbook may also benefit.

BEYOND BOOKBINDING Like many bookbinders, Joe Landau also sells books. Here again he praised the Internet as a forum where the customer can get an education in book collecting and the value of books. As a marketplace, the Internet has a leveling influence on the price of old books, he said, citing Advanced Book Exchange (www.abebooks.com) as an example of one such opportunity for the book-buying public. A Web site like Advanced Book Exchange's, with its thousands of dealers and millions of books, allows the public to compare with ease—what books are available, what prices dealers are asking for them. It's this factor that leads Joe to say that "individual dealers are no longer determining value. We were talking about *Huckleberry Finn*—a first edition, or a second edition. You see various dealers selling that same book at different prices. Let's say I had a first edition of a book, and there were only ten known copies. I could name my own price. But if you have ten different dealers competing to sell that book, then the fair market value will be averaged out." In the long run, Joe concluded, everyone concerned should benefit from the Internet as a book-selling medium. "All things being equal, it's a very democratic way of determining true value, true value being what the dealer wants to sell it for and what the customer wants to pay."

There remains the variable of book condition. Depending on how well and fully dealers describe the condition of each book they list on the Internet, and how well customers understand those details—dealer and buyer need to be on the same page, especially if it's foxed or loose—the Internet may be the endless bookshelf of a bibliomaniac's dreams. It cannot, however, give you the heft, texture, smell, and possible glow that come from holding a fine book in your hand and knowing that it's going home with you. And, if need be, on to a bookbinder for any care that you cannot, and should not, give it yourself.

(5)

HOW TO HOUSE AND
HANDLE BOOKS

Bookshelves and Bookends

W̶E knew of a dog whose sleeping arrangements were investigated after arthritis was diagnosed. The dog's human was stunned. She had crouched down in the breezeway where the dog had slept for years and found the space damp and unexpectedly cold at night. "I always kept it clean," she said of the dog's favorite spot, "but I'd never gotten down there to see what it was like. I had no idea. . . ."

Books don't develop arthritis, but they are prone to suffer from poor accommodations. While we don't ask that you spend a night on your bookshelves, there is much you can do to make sure that they would make you happy and secure if you were a book.

Books need shelves appropriate to their size (height and depth) and, in some cases, weight. It matters not at all whether the shelves are elaborate and custom-made or the old student standby: cinder block and unstained pine boards. Books are generally happier on unpainted surfaces. But what all shelves need to be is level.

Books should stand upright, resting on their bottom edges, in a straight vertical line.

If you have restricted shelf space and oversize books, there are special considerations. If a book must lie flat and horizontal, make sure it does so alone; no piling books up, one on another, no matter how attractive the arrangement.

Shelving an oversized book can create extra stress on the spine. If the book cannot stand vertically, shelve it with its fore edge down, but only as a last resort.

Also consider a book's edges. It goes without saying that edges will be damaged when a book is forced into space too short for its height. There are other hazards, too. If a shelf surface is rough, it may abrade the edge on which a book stands. Fore edges can be damaged—torn or indented—by having items stashed behind shelved books or where picture hooks or other items protrude from walls behind shelves.

Uneven pressure can distort the book's spine and warp the boards. Letting books lean also distorts, making bookends not only decorative but necessary.

Bookends come with their own caveats, of course. Avoid bookends with projections that slide under books. Best are bookends that are straight and solid where they meet their charges, and are heavy enough to keep books aligned like little soldiers on parade. Keep bookends, especially those with angled edges or irregular surfaces, away from books with leather bindings.

Allowing books to lean, forcing books into shelves too shallow for the books' height, and stacking books horizontally, especially atop vertically standing books (which permits uneven pressure to be exerted on the books), invite trouble. "Shaken" books, deformed and loose, their hinges failing, often emerge from cramped quarters or careless shelving. Shaken books tend to fall apart.

If you have glass-enclosed bookcases, remember to open them periodically to let air circulate around the books, dust the shelves and books regularly, and watch for musty odors. The same routine applies for books in any closed space, such as a cabinet, drawer, or closet.

Book Dummies

What happens when a book is removed from its shelf? A replacement, in shape if not in kind, should be available to fill the gap so that books still shelved do not tip and topple. Book dummies are the answer.

Library suppliers sell these book substitutes, made of such lightweight but sturdy substances as fiberboard. Most are manufactured with a spine label, which libraries use to note the title or location of a book absent from the shelf. You can ignore the label or use it as libraries do. Commercial book dummies are inexpensive, and are usually sold individually.

You can buy book dummies meant for library use and customize them, with fabric that matches your draperies or just about anything that appeals to you, as long as what you choose does not react with books. You might glue thumbnail-size photos or artwork clipped from magazines to the spine for a slim, vertical gallery. Used as they should be wherever books are active, book dummies will move around your shelves; think of them as roving decorative accents that help keep your books safe and your shelves orderly.

We've used various book-shaped objects to plug a hole in a shelf of books. A box of number 4 coffee filters did the job one day, and the post office's smallest Priority Mail carton, the one that's the size of a fat novel, another. A videocassette box also works, as does a vertical magazine file, a looseleaf binder, or any of scores of household objects. Only practicality need limit your imagination. You want only items that fill a book's space without being harmed themselves or harming an absent book's neighbors or the shelf.

If you dedicate a certain object to book dummydom, by all means make it as pretty as it is useful. The photos of book spines from a catalog or an anatomist's sketch of the bookworm might do the trick. If the latter interests you, try for a reproduction, from the *Micrographia* of 1665, of Hooke's splendid bookworm. A vertical rendering, it will fit a book dummy's spine, and the critter's image will certainly add interest to your shelves.

You can make personalized book dummies to give as gifts. Line the spines with snapshots of the kids, smiling as they peer over open books that the grandparents gave them, and you will make those grandparents smile, too.

Handling Books

-ᖰ-

Taking a book off a shelf is one of those automatic actions; we all do it, yet could we describe accurately how we do it?

As simple and repetitive (how could we do it wrong?!) as the task is, it bears thinking about. Think of it this way: If your dog developed a bad back from jumping up on and down off the bed, wouldn't you train the dog to wait to be lifted up and down, or throw out your bed and sleep on the floor with your dog? Of course you would.

From watching how people remove books from shelves, and quickly learning why some books need to be kept in locked cupboards, we began to watch ourselves, and draw useful conclusions.

Our preferred way of extracting a book from among others on a shelf is to approach the book we want laterally—slightly easing books on either side away from the one we want, just enough to slip our fingers around the desired book, grasping it by front and back covers, and pulling it straight out and off the shelf. This is another reason for giving books elbow room on shelves: your convenience. If you cannot easily insert your fingers around the book you want to retrieve, there are too many books on that shelf!

We may favor the lateral approach, but we have nothing but good things to say about the depth method, in which you slide books toward the back of the shelf in order to fetch the book you want. This works well when books sit forward on shelves, closer to you than to whatever is behind them, and on shelves that are deep.

Try to avoid tipping a book when you shelve or unshelve it; keeping it straight and level reduces edgewear.

By all means avoid removing a book from the shelf by pulling at the top of the spine. This can harm the hinge, tear the head of the spine, and create a nasty lasting scar.

Don't put things (except bookmarks; see next paragraph) inside books. Pressing a flower between pages may be romantic; it's also a chemical accident that begins the moment you close the book on that fresh-picked daisy and ends with the pages forever stained. Press and dry your keepsake flora elsewhere, and if you must keep it within the book for your own reasons, encase it in waxed paper or a glassine sleeve. If you like to save reviews of contemporary books or other clippings with the book they concern, the same routine applies: Place clippings in waxed paper or glassine sheaths, not between book pages. Remember that with few exceptions (such as keepsake books meant to house your mementos) books are designed and constructed to bear their own weight and maintain their own equilibrium. Compare a book with a packet of letters stuffed between its pages to a schoolchild stooped under a backpack. It works for a while, but presages trouble in the future.

What about bookmarks? By all means, mark your place with a bookmark, but the bookmark should be thin, and made of substances that in no way react with the book's paper. Indeed, "acid-free" should be emblazoned on any product that touches book paper. Many book professionals—binders, curators—favor leather bookmarks. The manufacturers of the Post-it note and its ilk market bookmarking tabs. Don't forget ribbon. Ribbon bookmarks were once an elegant built-in feature of many books.

A book could be written about the harm done to books by paperclips and staples. At the very least, a paperclip slipped over book pages will, when removed, leave its indented profile. At worst, and to the great detriment of older books, it will oxidize and leave an ugly, lasting stain. If you must leave papers in a book, remove any fasteners. It takes amazingly little humidity to turn them into hole-borers and tear-inciters.

Gloves: If you have especially fragile books (such as delicate fabric bindings) or ephemera, keep curator's gloves on hand. You can order them from the library suppliers listed on pages 160–64, and you'll probably find that they are useful in many tasks unrelated to books. As much as possible, spare fine old books from the natural oils of the human hand and what the hand may transmit (bacteria that might react on the book's constituents as well as residue of food and toiletries).

Now that the book is off the shelf, it begs to be opened. Here, too, there are basic courtesies. Deference to the book's backbone, the spine, requires no deep bends: Never force a book past the 180 degree point of lying open flat, and *never* place an open book pages down. Clever and attractive devices—small book weights available commercially—can safely hold a book open for you; your coffee cup and saucer were not designed for this task.

Remember that many old books will not lie open because they're bound too tightly. This is the difference between Smyth (rhymes with "blithe") sewn books and side-sewn books. Smyth sewn books are sewn with thread along the folds of the signature, and then each signature is attached to the next; this allows the book pages to lie flat while keeping the individual signatures together. Side-sewn books are sewn from the side through all the individual leaves at one time; this makes for a strong book but does not allow the book to lie flat. To force such a book to lie flat is to risk serious structural damage.

Opening a New Book
꒦

A new book needs a good stretch. We've often likened it to a dog getting out of bed in the morning, not with a bound and a leap but with a leisurely extension of spine and limbs, and a satisfied wag of the tail.

If the book is wearing a jacket, slip it off before the exercise session. Stand the book on its spine and allow the covers to fold open. Grasp the text block in one hand; the book's contents should be standing up straight above the spine. With the fingertips of the other hand (or a blunt instrument such as the bone folder), press gently along the hinges of each cover. The hinges under the endpapers protrude a half an inch or so (depending on the size of the book) from the spine onto the boards.

Next, break in the text block. From the front of the book, take several pages—as many as ten or twelve—and press them down gently while supporting the bulk of the text block as you did while breaking in the hinges. Move to the back of the book, and repeat the process. Return to the front of the book, and break in the next several pages. Continue, back and forth from the front and back of the block, until you have worked your way through the entire book.

This kind of intimate handling of a new book not only readies it for reading. It may also show you that the book is so finely made, its dust jacket so attractive, that you want to take immediate steps to safeguard its future.

Extra Protection for Individual Books
⌄

Clear, thin, and more flexible than paper, synthetics are ideal for extra protection. Use these for your most precious books, or your most active (no cookbook should enter the kitchen without one).

There are book jacket covers, available in premeasured, exact sizes, into which the jacket issued with the book can easily be slipped. There are also adjustable book jacket covers. Which to choose? It's a matter of personal preference. To decide which is best for you, consider the sizes of your books (are they all of the most popular standard measurements or of unusual dimensions?) and, to some extent, manual dexterity. You don't need much of the latter, but more is better when covers need adjustment.

These suits of transparent armor guard against fingerprints, dust, abrasions and tears, spills and other stains, and most of all, water. They can be wiped clean with rubbing alcohol when they do become soiled.

Extra protection also comes in bulk, on rolls like bolts of fabric. In this form, the covering can be cut to any book's precise specifications, and can be formed, using a bone, to fit securely.

There are also self-adhesive laminates you can use to cover paperbacks or other items worth preserving.

On older books, these coverings can also act as a cosmetic, masking imperfections and making the overall book look better. Acid-free synthetics protect leather bindings against red rot, which occurs when leather deteriorates.

Books with dust jackets: Library and archival suppliers sell clear jackets in a variety of styles and sizes. They are sold in quantity, are available in assortments of various exact and adjustable sizes, and come with instructions. Among the many precise sizes, the eight- to fourteeninchers are the ones most personal libraries need. Some suppliers offer extra-long sizes suitable for oversized books.

There are numerous variations. Some jacket covers feature a paper liner, not visible when the cover is in place, which supports the dust jacket it preserves. The paper liner can be a godsend to a dust jacket that is chipped or torn. Covers without the paper liner are usually less expensive, and more than adequate for new dust jackets that have not seen much wear. Most jackets are secured by means of adhesive-bearing tabs or continuous strips, which make application easy.

Book jacket covers are made of several substances. These include Melinex 516 (DuPont's polyester film that has replaced the long-established Mylar for archival use), polyester (strong, chemically stable, and acid-free; also appropriate for archival use), and polypropylene (more flexible than the preceding two substances, but acid-free and stable). The covers are also made in different mils (a mil equals one one-thousandth of an inch), giving heft as well as protection. For general use, 1.5 mils is adequate; consider 2 mils on more-precious or delicate books.

The covers are manufactured in several finishes. Choose clear styles when you want maximum transparency; these make books shine. The low-glare, nonglare, and slightly textured matte finishes may be what you want for certain books, to detract from imperfections or to conform to your aesthethic sense—an early twentieth-century dust jacket in perfect repair might look more becoming to you in a nonreflective cover. There are some situations, usually related to light, in which books may fare better in covers of one finish or another. The book you plan to read on the beach for a week deserves the equivalent of your sunscreen and broad-brimmed straw hat. Some suppliers make jackets that inhibit ultraviolet rays and are perfect for books that can't be protected against fading from fluorescent lamps or sun exposure.

We favor jackets such as Brodart's acid-free "Just-A-Fold," which encases a dust jacket in seconds. It has clear polyester on one side, and blank white paper on the other. As its name implies, this jacket is easy to adjust for a perfect fit. The adjustment is a simple matter of lining up the book's own dust jacket with the clear addition, and making a crisp, straight fold or two.

When a dust jacket's size does not correspond with a precut cover, choose a clear cover that is larger than the dust jacket, and fold the plastic smaller until it fits. A dust jacket cramped by plastic that's too tight will eventually wrinkle, giving the book an overall shabby appearance.

You can also cover a dust jacket with a single sheet of one of the clear film products, treating it as if it were an unjacketed book (see next paragraph).

Books without dust jackets: Were you one of those kids who covered school books with plain brown wrapping paper? We remember it well, how we would fold the paper to fit the book, making flaps that wrapped around the book's covers.

No matter how fine the workmanship, the brown paper obscures art and other information on a book's boards. Unless disguising the book is the point, a clear polyester film product is the best choice.

1. Cut the film to the exact height of the book you want to protect. Optional: Cut the film a little longer for extra protection.
2. Cut the film to approximately three times the width of a slender book, four times the width of a thick book.
3. Wrap the film around the book so that the ends of the film meet.
4. Note (with a light crease) or mark (with pen or pencil) the position of creases, where the film will wrap around the book's covers, creating the end flaps. You can crease the film easily with a ruler or bone folder. A spot of rubbing alcohol will remove any pen or pencil

marks made during measuring. Then fold the creased film over the boards.

Remembering Mylar: Over its long and useful life, Mylar was so identified with book jacket covers that the name became all but synonymous with them, just as "Kleenex" has been used often for any and all facial tissues. You may see mentions in dealers' descriptions on the Internet or in catalogs of a book that is "Mylared" or "in Mylar" (though not everyone grants the product its rightful initial cap). This recognition may need adjustment, just like some of the jacket covers that are made of it. For Mylar was discontinued in the spring of 2001, replaced for use in the graphic arts industry by Melinex 516. (Mylar is still on the job, however; it protected the windows of the U.S. Capitol since the fall of 2001, and has been mentioned as part of Earth's future defense against asteroids.) We will be sorry to see the Mylar name, symbolic to us of improved stock and happier customers, fade from the world of books, if indeed it does. The name alone may inspire book people to be possessive of it, in defiance of progress. Perhaps we will dedicate a corner of one bookshelf to the name, near our shrine to the pica and printer's ink.

A Library Supplier's Advice
⁓

Despite their concentration on institutions, library suppliers serve the individual book owner, too. Don't worry about quantities when ordering; you can order from these companies without making purchases to last a lifetime.

Book jacket covers are commonly sold in units of twenty-five or fifty pieces, which the average bookcase will absorb in no time.

Most of all, don't worry that you won't know what to ask. Just know what you hope to accomplish. The salespeople know what to ask you.

Patty Leidhecker, director of product management at Brodart's McElhattan, Pennsylvania, offices, told us that while individual customers account for only 1 or 2 percent of the company's overall sales, those customers and their special needs are understood. Telephone and Internet staff recognize the potential for confusion when customers browse the printed catalog (the 2001 edition had 654 pages) or the online version; not only are there many products, there are variations on the many products.

Book jacket covers are what most individuals buy, Patty said, adding that Brodart staff ask if there are old books to be cared for, books with dust jackets, books without jackets. "There are certain questions we have to ask so we can narrow it down to a few styles. Are you looking for exact fit, or are you looking for something that you're willing to do a little bit of folding on. Exact fit is a little bit more expensive. Are you budget-conscious? You can go back and forth on that."

Asked what she would most like to convey to the individual book owner, Patty was quick to reply. "Protect it, as soon as you get it. Don't wait." Many people, she explained, wait until they discover their collections growing by leaps and bounds. "Whether you're a beginner or you have a collection, get them under wraps ASAP. Start with your basic book jacket cover, and then, obviously, if you need to do some repairs, do it."

Old books with dust jackets are a special case. Patty recommends that their owners fit them for nonglare, archival-quality protection. "Archival meaning that it's pH neutral, the adhesive that's used on it is acid-free as well, and there's no printing on the paper [liner], so ink won't migrate into the book itself."

Long-term Storage
꘎

If you must store books in boxes, keep in mind that the best of intentions can have poor consequences. Professional movers and suppliers of moving paraphernalia offer cartons suitable for books. Such cartons are usually on the small side, as well they should be. We like a well-constructed (note how many have reinforced seams), clean, dry liquor carton for books. Books are heavier than you think they are, especially in quantity. The heavier the box of books, in our experience, the more likely it is to be dropped or otherwise abused. Books may not be as fragile as a dozen eggs, but they are susceptible to injury.

Try not to stuff too many books into too few boxes. When packing books for long journeys, a pecking order is bound to emerge: Give your precious hardcover books individual wrappers (the traditional sturdy plain brown wrapping paper, tissue paper, bubble wrap, or waxed paper will do the trick and keep books from chafing each other in transit), and make tidy bundles of a few same-sized paperbacks. Books should not be able to bounce or shift in their cartons.

You can wrap books in clean newspapers for a short period of time—during a move, for example. Be careful not to transfer printer's ink from your hands to the books; wear gloves when you handle newsprint. It's wise not to store books wrapped in newsprint for longer periods; the paper can be acidic and in time damage your library.

You can store books in clean plastic bags, too, but not for long. If there is the slightest moisture or mold present when you bag your books, trouble will brew. Always prick a plastic bag that holds a book.

Avoid storage in attics and basements, unless they are climate-controlled. Even if those spaces have heat and air-conditioning, they may be worth avoiding for books' sake. By the time you discover that the roof is leaking or that the cellar has flooded, it may be too late. Boxed books should sit on pallets, never on the floor, and far from, or at least shielded from, sprinkler heads.

When you rent space for books in a self-service storage facility, ask for a unit on a middle floor, and one in the middle of the structure. The idea is to be as far away from the pests and perils of the outside world as possible. Whether your books remain in cartons or stand on shelves in storage, consider draping some plastic sheeting over the cartons (which, of course, will not sit directly on the floor but on pallets) or loosely cover the shelves.

If your books are going into storage at a commercial warehouse, ask the proprietors about temperature and humidity. Do they recommend a particular type of container for books, especially if their premises are sprinklered?

A final thought: Pack your books yourself. The more books you own, the more you need an inventory. Code each carton, with numbers, letters, or any other nonrepeating device. Then, in a notebook that will be stowed with your passport and will, list the contents of each carton. Do you have just a few books on a given subject? Then "radiometry" or "holothurians" or even "whatever" may suffice. More than a few books on a subject, and more detail will help you one day. Author surnames may be enough to identify your books to you, or you may need a formal roster done in bibliographic style. Sounds tedious, perhaps, but it's all a good investment in time and effort.

Packing and Shipping
⚜

If there's a present nicer than a book, to give or receive, we haven't heard of it. "The right book at the right time," wrote *Los Angeles Times* columnist and author Lee Shippey in the 1930s, "may mean more in a person's life than anything else."

If you're the giver of such a wonderful gift, and must ship the book to its recipient, here are some guidelines to help the book arrive safely.

The first rule: A book must be wrapped before it travels. Use tissue paper, thin bubble wrap, newsprint-weight paper sold at many office supply shops, or gift wrap. Archival suppliers sell acid-free tissue paper that protects fine bindings from the hazards of other packing materials and the travel environment; it can also be useful in storing delicate paper treasures around the house.

Don't have anything that resembles traditional wrapping paper? Tape two or more sheets of paper together—bond paper from your printer, sheets from a legal pad. Use clean sheets of paper; ink or crayon or other materials may be transferred to certain book surfaces. A simple paper bag, assuming it's clean and dry, can be cut to wrap a book. The paper that drapes dry cleaning or professionally laundered articles can do the trick. We don't approve of wrapping books in paper towels or facial tissues, but only because so many of those products contain additives that are fine when you dry your hands or pat your nose: aloe vera, vitamin E, fragrances, and the like.

Are you enclosing something with the book? A greeting card in an envelope probably will not damage the average book, so if you prefer to place an envelope inside a book's initial wrapping, we won't rap your knuckles. There are common items—paper clips, staples, and other fasteners—that can gouge, scratch, scrape, and tear. These must be separated from any book by stout wrapping paper.

Shipping more than one book in the same parcel? Each individual book needs its own wrapper. Some books, such as two or three same-sized paperbacks once each has been wrapped separately, travel well bundled together before further wrapping. The more delicate the book, the more that can go wrong with it, the more individual wrapping it needs before it rubs shoulders, and spines, in a box with other books.

There are book professionals—including publishers, wholesalers, distributors, and booksellers—who ship books without wrapping, padding, or protection of any kind. (The shrinkwrap often used on individual or bundled books looks more impressive than it is; it may keep dust jackets from tearing but it never yet prevented bumped corners.) We recall a carton received from a publisher one day; of the twenty-nine new books inside, eight were in salable condition. The carton contained nothing but books, and plenty of space for them to bounce, collide, and maul each other, and they had had a field day. (The order's packing slip, in a snug waterproof sheath, was in pristine condition.) All who contribute to such carelessness (and consequent false economy), from policy-makers to packers, are bound for merchant purgatory, where they will always receive everything they want—damaged.

The second rule: A book should not be able to shift in its wrappings during transit. When you ship a book in a box, make sure the box is sufficiently larger than the book. Larger than the book does not mean that the book fits inside the box, or that the box fits around the book. The book and the box should not meet. (You can, of course, pack a book in a small box inside a larger box. Even so, leave room for some padding around the smaller container.)

By "sufficiently larger" we mean that once a book, in its initial wrapper and the heavier layer of protective wrapping over that, is placed in the box, there is space to fill with plenty of padding. The book sits not on the bottom of the box but on resilient packing material: crumpled newspaper, packing pellets, layers of bubble wrap. As you look down into the carton at the wrapped book, can you see space (at least an inch, or three centimeters, is ideal) on all four sides? Once the book is resting on the packing material underneath it, it's time to tuck it in—as you would tuck up a baby in its crib or a puppy in its basket, not with blankets or your old sweater but with lengths of crumpled newspaper or scraps of bubble wrap. When the box is closed, it should touch, not the wrapped book, but the packing material placed atop it.

The heavier the book, the more room you should allow for resilient padding: bubble wrap, crumpled newspaper, packing pellets. An unusually heavy book or one that is fragile will benefit from cardboard or Styrofoam layers between whatever wraps the book itself and the resilient matter that surrounds it in the carton. Regardless of what surrounds it, the book itself needs careful, snug wrapping.

If you have gift-wrapped a book prior to shipping, by all means protect the gift wrap with a plastic bag or a layer of bubble wrap. Then wrap the bagged book in several sheets of newspaper or bubble wrap.

Once the book is wrapped, packed, and its carton sealed securely with a heavy-duty tape, there's one last worthwhile task. Reinforce all carton edges with a heavy-duty sealing tape. Helping the carton keep its shape helps the book travel safely.

If you know something about conditions at the book's destination—if parcels are left on an open front porch, and it's monsoon season, the snow is drifting, or if insects are a nuisance—take an additional precaution. Enclose the wrapped book in a plastic bag or other water-resistant covering; check for holes or weakening seams and seal before placing it, with ample padding, in its carton. Remember that bubble wrap with perforated seams may not create a watertight shield. An alternative is to strap the entire box with overlapping strips of heavy-duty sealing tape. The result may not be technically waterproof, but it will certainly protect the contents against a brief downpour or a few minutes on wet pavement.

The third rule: When shipping a book in an envelope, even one of the padded variety or one lined with bubble wrap, take extra precautions. Once the book is wrapped, cut cardboard slightly larger than the book. We like the weight and durability of liquor cartons' cardboard, and that of other heavy-duty shipping boxes. The cardboard must be clean and dry, thick and unbending. Place the book between the cardboard sheets, and secure them with tape for extra reinforcement. Now, wrap the cardboard-secured book in another layer of wrapping, such as several sheets of newspaper. Try the envelope on for size, and if the wrapped book moves, take it out and wrap it again. Keep wrapping the cardboard-protected book until it fits snugly and does not move in the envelope.

Don't forget to protect your shipping labels against accident. Labels can experience fatal adhesive failure, or just get torn off. An address can get wet and illegibile. A layer of clear heavy-duty tape should protect your return address and the recipient's.

The fourth and final rule: If a shipped book is easy to unwrap, it's not wrapped properly!

(6)

REFLECTING ON BOOKS

The more furiously and prodigiously books are put in circulation, the more fluently will they pass into the arteries of the
second-hand trade; this is where the real glamour of books has
its color and essence. In those dim aisles of dusty brethren,
books come to their just level. Their sins and sorrows are upon
them; they are no longer bricks of merchandize [sic] but human
emanations of triumph or disappointment. They are no longer
merely property; they become audible as a voice from another
world.   —*The Book Dial*
                                                          DECEMBER 1923

ONE day a visitor to our shop browsed a while and
then asked us, quite pointedly, why we had so many
old books. It was the first time we had been asked to jus-
tify the presence of old books among the new. We wanted
to offer the best books we could find, we said. We
explained that we often suggest an older dog book over a
newer title; an older book may better address a specific

interest, it may be better written or more beautiful to look at and handle. We recommend older books for variety, for a perspective from another time, or for a glimpse of some aspect of the dog world that may be gone forever. New books, we added, are not necessarily better than older ones, not in content, not in construction. We didn't think of it at the time, but might have quoted Quercus: "Be bold, be bold . . . but not too bold; among new books buy something old."

What prompted the question? The visitor wanted only the very latest books, and told us that the sight of old books, often more expensive than the new ones with which they were shelved, was none too reassuring.

Our visitor was, like us, as happy to go off on a tangent as on holiday, so we soon knew all about the dogs at home, ranging in age from a few months to the mid-teens. Did all those "new and old" dogs live and play together, we asked? They did, and happily, we were told.

Something else dogs and books share, we thought; the old and new together, thriving. Then off we went on another tangent: What constitutes an old book?

It might simply be a book that is older than we are, or older than you are. Or it may be old according to scholarly or commercial rubrics. An old book is not always valuable, but many are worth a great deal of money. There are used and secondhand books, lowly remainders, and so on, up the scale to the collector's copies and the scarce and exceedingly rare. The classifications vary, depending on the source; it's much like pondering the domestic dog's varieties.

We've often heard the love of old books compared to the appreciation of fine wines. Rare vintages are worth cherishing; fine old books, we believe, are their readable equals. But you can drink the wine once only.

Then again, some wines turn to vinegar. And some books turn to dust.

We would never disparage vinegar; we would report that it is no longer what it once was. Something similar happens to books. There may be the unambiguous end inflicted by fire or water. There's the culling that occurs for a host of reasons, including a strange affliction known by its helpless victims as "too many books." Lesser accidents and the aging process can also contribute to a book's demise.

Two questions arise: How do you decide if a book's life is over, and how do you dispense with books?

A book lover knows when a book has, in effect, died. For the passionate book soul, the discovery is less devastating but just as real, and comes from the same unplumbed source, as another terrible understanding: A beloved pet's life is approaching its end.

When a book has been damaged beyond repair: If your reverence for books demands it, or a book has been an especially close friend, keep a title page or illustration or some portion as a keepsake, and let the remains be recycled. Perhaps its essence will be revived in another book that will make someone happier or wiser.

When your reasons for parting with books have little or nothing to do with the books' condition: Setting books out with the trash strikes us as an ignominious end. Donate your books to a charity, a thrift shop, or bazaar;

you'll be doing a good deed and may earn a tax deduction. Books in good condition might be welcome at a hospital, school, or other community institution.

Contact dealers of secondhand books, or purveyors of rare books if your collection warrants. The *Yellow Pages* of your phone book can help you find nearby dealers who may be as delighted to accept your books as you are to part with them. To help dealers decide whether to make you an offer, make a list of the books you want to sell (author, title, illustrator, publisher, and year are crucial), with a brief report on the condition of each.

There are no absolute guidelines for describing book condition. Well-intentioned sellers disagree, making one person's volume in good condition look poor to fair to someone else. By all means, give your opinion, but focus on particulars: Is the dust jacket present? Is it price-clipped? Are there any inscriptions or marginalia in the book? Is all artwork intact?

The Internet offers many ways of selling, auctioning, or donating books. Indeed, the Internet allows anyone to become a book dealer. If you hope to sell your books, remember that condition is an important factor. All the more reason to repair and care for your books!

Book Collecting
꘍

You can collect books on any subject, including book collecting itself. Time, subject, shelf space, and budget may set limits for you. But nothing diminishes the challenge and sheer fun of the hunt.

You can collect old books as an investment, out of a general love of old things, or a need for books unavailable in any but old editions. Old books survive in the strangest places. It may be less likely as time goes by to rescue a fine volume from a street table laden with romance paperbacks, but it can happen. Never stop looking.

Book collecting is by no means limited to old books. Which books among recent releases will become the foundations of twenty-first century literary collections?

No matter what you collect or why, ask yourself some questions about your collection from time to time. Which of your books would you like your grandchildren to have? You may one day need or want to sell some or all of your books. By your choice or happenstance, your books may someday be someone else's. Take care of those books now.

That care extends beyond proper housing and maintenance for your books to personalization. Many people add bookplates or marginal notes. There are still dedicated grangerizers, too. Books meant as gifts are often inscribed to recipients, and preprinted prices on dust jacket flaps are often clipped. Remember that every such alteration to a book affects its value.

Borrowing and Lending
↯

There is a passage in *The Haunted Bookshop* of Christopher Morley that ought to hang near every bookcase, next to a cautionary noose. Its message in defense of books may keep peace among friends, prolong family ties, and aid in the propagation of good book manners and general civility:

> I give hearty and humble thanks for the safe return of this book, which having endured the perils of my friend's bookcase and the bookcases of my friend's friends, now returns to me in reasonably good condition. I give hearty and humble thanks that my friend did not see fit to give this book to his infant for a plaything, nor use it as an ash tray for his burning cigar, nor as a teething ring for his mastiff. When I loaned this book, I deemed it as lost; I was resigned to the business of the long parting; I never thought to look upon its pages again. But now that my book has come back to me, I rejoice and am exceedingly glad! Bring hither the fatted morocco and let us rebind the volume and set it on the shelf of honor, for this my book was lent and is returned again. Presently, therefore, I may return some of the books I myself have borrowed.

Children and Old Books

꙳

Children and dogs are perfect together. Children and books are a wonderful pairing, too. Even better: children and dogs, curled up with books. That's near perfection, improvable only by making the books old ones.

There is the obvious reason: Some remarkable children's books are out of print. How many of us treasure, as adults, books we were given as youngsters, including books that were old even then? And that remain part of the memory of loved ones who gave them to us, or a link with times or places we remember dimly or not at all.

Many young readers are receptive to old books. Sometimes a book's age itself piques curiosity. Why not promote an interest in the past with a tangible link to it? Think of all the wonderful old books about the future. Kids will enjoy those, too.

Children may be just as perceptive as dogs are, and many kids are probably just as tenacious. We all want children to love books. So if a child is old enough to be aware of a book, and for some reason you must dispose of that book, we have a suggestion: Don't let a child pine for and perhaps search like a frustrated puppy for a missing treasure. Tell the child what's happening to the book and why, and replace the book with a copy of the same title or something new to suggest continuity and a sense that the world is full of stories and pictures.

You might even conduct a little ceremony, in which you and the child say thank you and good-bye to the book.

(But what if a child has, as many do, drawn or scrawled or written in a book—perhaps first practiced the alphabet or his or her name—how can one part with it? Unless the book has been spoiled by fire or water, it must be kept. At least until the child is old enough, and has voted in half a dozen presidential elections, to decide that the book is no longer wanted. The late Dr. Mitzi Myers, scholar of children's literature, believed that in what children do to their books we can find "the hidden history of childhood." Isn't that worth preserving?)

The idea of the parting ceremony comes from our German shorthaired pointer Po, in whose life "the ball" was central. Before we knew better, when we thought the dog wouldn't notice—for we lived surrounded by tennis balls, once counting eighty-three in the living room alone—we disposed of worn, skinless balls whenever it was convenient for us. But Po knew every tennis ball intimately; each was precious, its condition irrelevant. Whenever a ball went missing, his brilliant investigative nose found it. He would lead us to the garbage pail. He would demonstrate that he knew better than to overturn the garbage pail, that to commit such a breach of dog manners would pain him, but he was capable of it and, with a tennis ball at stake, morally justified. We would retrieve the tossed-out ball, apologize, let him examine it, and then together we would replace it in the trash. Po forgave us often, always with kisses and a wagging tail. Finally we learned: It was only fair to do what we wanted *his* way.

Now whenever Rose the dachshund skins a tennis ball, she escorts it to the trash can. We say thank you and farewell. Rose is pleased to accept a new ball, and life goes on.

Sociable Book Care

If you belong to a reading group, you have the beginning of your guest list. Or invite everyone you know. Learn the truth about people, or just how much they love books. The occasion? A book cleaning and repair party.

Each guest might bring five books, and everybody can kibitz over the books' problems and what can or should be done to each one. Then parcel out the tasks according to each guest's talents. Some people are born to handle fine-grain sandpaper (that's your friend the cabinetmaker), others are born to glue (it's been said that orthopedic surgeons make good book doctors).

As host, you should provide some basic repair and cleaning supplies, perhaps some clear book jackets, too. Refreshments should be served, but not near the work area; crumb cake and adhesives have a way of meeting in the strangest places. Offer a door prize (the classic five-hundred-piece after-dinner set, or a box of toothpicks, always gets a laugh, but a book on books might be appreciated just as much). As you and your guests look to the future—for no first book care party is ever the last—why not decide on themes? Cookbook or children's book repair next time, or the anniversary of the first dated book printed in England, which William Caxton issued in November 1477. Or take your party on the road as a civic pleasure (does your library or school need your book care services?). Pooling skills and interests can make the repair you've been hesitating to do alone proceed expeditiously when there are like-minded souls and a little debate to back you up. Pool pocketbooks, too, and buy dust jacket covers and other items in quantity. Your group might even grant an honorary title or two. Not everyone needs access to a stinky book box every day; appoint someone keeper of the stinky book box, which may be used between gatherings by appointment.

Before dismissing the book care party idea as only an attempt at humor, remember that people will do in groups what they will not do as individuals. A book care party lets you and other book lovers do together with a chuckle what you might each face alone with a frown.

A Gift of Book Care
❦

Do you know someone whose books need attention—from a simple dusting to some routine repairs—but who is unable to do the work for some reason? If you would fetch milk or the mail for that person, why not offer to dust the books and shelves and clean and repair some of the books? "May I clean your books?" may sound like an odd offer, but it can be made in a way that makes people smile and accept.

There's no reason to limit your gift of book care to someone who is physically unable to do the job. What a nice holiday or birthday surprise it might be for someone you know who would love to have spruced and dusted books, but never gets around to it.

What of people who are capable of giving books needed care but are disinclined? In this situation, you are friend not to the person but to the books, their advocate. You might offer to show how the work is done (shame still works wonders on some people) or volunteer to adopt the books that are in the neglectful owner's way.

At the Library
❦

What is life like for the average circulating library book?

Curious, we asked public libraries throughout the United States—in many of the largest metropolises and many more smaller cities and towns—how they care for books that people borrow. By telephone and e-mail, and in visits to branch libraries in our home borough of Manhattan, we asked librarians what happens when circulating books get hurt. We asked what they tell borrowers about the care and handling of library books. We asked if they educate the public about how to keep books alive. We toured dozens of public library Web sites, found them brimming with information about everything but what we wanted to know: the intimate life of circulating books.

On balance, our investigations brought us closer than we had ever been to the essence of the proverbial second prize. For we learned that, more often than not, a circulating book's lot is not a happy one. It is one that a concerned library patron—anyone who has cherished borrowed books or has been dependent for knowledge or diversion on a circulating library—might want to see amended.

We cannot emphasize enough that our casual survey was devoted to circulating books (rare books and reference materials are generally well treated). We queried only a minuscule number of the approximately 16,000 public libraries (a figure encompassing central libraries and branches) in the United States, which has more than 122,000 libraries—public, school, academic, armed forces, government, and specialized (such as law or music or medicine)—as enumerated by the American Library Association. There's a phrase in that organization's formal policy on preservation—"usability, durability, and longevity"—that certainly was not inspired by the average circulating library book. Fair enough perhaps, in an imperfect world. But it was from an imperfect world that today's rare books emerged, and few if any of them were created rare. How many of today's new books, and tomorrow's, will get their crack at immortality? That we are all going to die is no excuse to die young.

What happens when circulating books need repair? In general, the libraries we queried do little to remedy everyday wear and tear to circulating books. Many librarians spoke of what one called "meatball surgery"—the occasional use of glue and tape. Professional care is usually reserved for rare books and reference volumes.

When libraries do repair circulating books, they call upon a range of services, from the occasional volunteer to a full-time staff, doing the work on the premises or having it done at a central library system facility or a commercial bindery.

Even libraries that said they could repair circulating books admitted that often they did not. Many discard a book rather than make a simple repair; they prefer to buy a new copy and insist that this policy makes good financial sense. To rebind a book generally costs more than buying a new copy of the same book.

However, suppose a new copy of a book cannot be obtained, for budgetary reasons or because it's out of print; libraries certainly buy out-of-print books, but such books cannot always be located—sometimes not quickly, sometimes not at all—and can be expensive. Why should a book become unavailable to a library's public simply because a copy that could be repaired has been allowed to deteriorate, and to be discarded for neglect?

To repair circulating books is not cost-effective, we were told time and again. It's a waste of time, and if it weren't a waste of time, staffing constraints prevent it. Even if there were personnel whose time could be scheduled for routine repair, library people rarely have the basic training they would need to do the job, we were told. In a way, then, it's a good thing that it makes no economic sense.

(So many library people spoke of cost-effectiveness that we suddenly wondered if we were fools to clean and repair the books we sell. Were we wasting our time to earn a bit more on the sale of each improved book? Which assumes that each such book would sell as quickly in its unimproved state; knowing how important condition is to most of our customers, we would be ashamed and stupid to offer books in conditions poorer than need be. We decided to test the premise. We took a whole shelf of books that needed basic cleaning and modest repairs and set to work, noting the time work began and the time work ended. We spent more time on the arithmetic that reassured us than we did on some of the individual repairs: We spent only a few minutes on each task per book. It seems that our time is well invested, even when time equals money. We get some satisfaction from it, too, and our customers get better merchandise.)

What do libraries tell borrowers about the care and handling of library books? Do libraries educate the public about how to keep books alive? We found libraries whose staff lectured on rare books or special collections, but never said a word about mundane books and their care.

How many of those rare books and volumes in special collections that are fit lecture topics now were, when new, ordinary and unpromising?

Of the institutions that repair circulating books, not one said they had ever let the public in on its secrets: not a single lecture or workshop or bring-your-hurt-book event. Not a page on a Web site, or a yearly talk by a librarian or bookbinder, not a simple printed fact sheet to hand out, or advice posted for all library visitors to see.

It was at this point in our conversations with some pleasant and intelligent library professionals that we often heard ambivalence and disdain. People who borrow books are not serious readers, we were told. People who use the library don't care about books. People who borrow books are careless. People who use the library can't be taught anything. In short, public libraries can and will tell you more about how to recycle a milk carton (a disposable item) than how to treat a circulating book that should have a long shelf life.

Indeed, few libraries told us that they print anything for the public, other than a schedule of hours or events. The New York Public Library is one of the few. Its pamphlet called "Rules & Regulations" devotes almost two of its seven columns to a code of behavior with which "the public is required to comply." Forbidden acts include "standing idly about" and "lingering aimlessly"—whether one may do either with a book in hand, or while thinking, is not made plain, an oversight that makes us nervous. The city's library system, with its more than ten million books, prints only thirteen words to guide us in our conduct with what we borrow from it: "Please take good care of the library materials and property that you use."

Why doesn't the library's pamphlet say something specific about the "good care" library books deserve, and how to provide it? It warns against and cites penalties for damaging library property; New York State Education Law, Section 264, is ready for each infraction. There are care and use instructions on circulating videotapes and other electronic media. Why don't a few words of positive advice accompany each book?

Should we challenge the conditions in which most circulating library books live? We think it's worth a try.

What we propose may have all the charm of lancing a dinner guest's boil—but done between courses, with discretion and a nod to hygiene, it could save the evening. This unappetizing vision—an attention-getter, and vulgar—appeals to us for one simple reason. If we take care of our books, those in our home or business, we ought to take care of our books in our public libraries, which, when we borrow them, are our guests. The public is us. Those books are ours. Many of those books need basic attention that they are not getting, and is there anything more vulgar than neglect? What ails circulating library books is not going to go away—the books will be discarded far more often than they are fixed. You may have raised money for your local library's new wing, chaired the spring gala, fed the visiting author, helped with the bake sale or the literacy program, read to the children, or judged their short story or scarecrow contest. You have done all the obvious, organized, and admirable things;

you have shown your support. Yet you haven't done the unexciting thing, or helped the individual for whom the library is home: You have not assisted a single book that may need minor but life-saving attention.

Have you asked if your library needs help dusting the shelves, or checking for signs of pests in the stacks? Could you refresh book jacket covers with a cloth and rubbing alcohol? Replace torn book jacket covers? Mend torn endpapers?

You might start the next time you return a book to the library—or just before. Are there fingerprints or food spots on the book jacket cover? Take a cloth and some rubbing alcohol and tidy up after yourself. You will have added to the book's appeal to its next reader, and, perhaps, to its circulating life. Think of it as you might about a public campsite or picnic ground, or the way we do about Central Park: Always leave it a little cleaner than you found it.

We envision something primarily civil. Not community-minded, but book-minded. Not a speech but a conversation. It would need no by-laws or meetings, attorneys or acronyms. It could function on the occasional phone call, casual remark, or moment's inspiration. It might be founded when you ask your local librarian if the library has any books that are no longer circulating because of minor damage. It might begin its worthwhile work, and record its first accomplishment, when the librarian shows you a soiled or wounded book and you say, "I can fix that!" As you would at home, match the library book's condition to the care and repair recommendations in this book. Do only to library property what you would do for your own.

Who might be willing to participate? Anyone who has the slightest sense of gratitude to libraries. Who remembers benefitting—laughing, crying, winning an argument, making a living—from the reading of a book found only in a library? Suppose that book had not been available because it had had an easily reparable injury and instead of repair it got the axe?

If solitary volunteerism doesn't appeal to you, order T-shirts or aprons that say something like "A Book's Best Friends" and invite your friends for a little bit of an adventure. If you belong to a reading group, perhaps all of you could devote a few hours periodically to book care at your local library. Such a group might be self-taught and work under a sympathetic librarian's supervision. Or you might find a mentor—a retired bookbinder, perhaps—who is happy to impart some knowledge and guide your efforts.

To the objection that you are not a librarian or other book professional, you will be well equipped. You will have cleaned or mended some books at home; bring them to the library as your references. Offer to provide your own care-and-repair supplies. Or engage in an act of daring: Enter your library with clean lint-free cloths and rubbing alcohol, identify needy books, and begin to clean them. Remember that it's not just that those who can't do, teach; many of those who can't or won't do don't believe anyone else can, will, or should either. Prove them wrong!

You can always describe how, with no medical degree but only a first-aid manual and a few items from your bathroom cabinet, you lanced the dinner guest's boil and, moments later, served to acclaim nothing less than madeleines, which, of course, you will bake by the dozens in time for the library's next fund-raiser.

The Future of Books

❧

We often recall a chat that made us shudder. A woman described how she had recently moved into an old house in New England and discovered cupboards and an attic full of nineteenth-century books—hundreds of them, she said. Then she sighed. There had been so much to do, with renovations and the kids adjusting to a new community, that when the Dumpster was delivered she had had the books tossed into it with the old floorboards and plaster. She was full of regret, and often imagined, she told us, what books she might have had. It was a sad story of books lost to haste. Books disappear that and other ways every day.

"To acquire the habit of reading is to construct for yourself a refuge from almost all the miseries of life." W. Somerset Maugham's observation expands whenever people to whom it is truth construct a refuge for the books they love.

The English printer and bibliographer William Blades, writing in the nineteenth century, said:

It is a great pity that there should be so many distinct enemies at work for the destruction of literature, and that they should so often be allowed to work out their sad end. Looked at rightly, the possession of any old book is a sacred trust, which a conscientious owner or guardian would as soon think of ignoring as a parent would of neglecting his child. An old book, whatever its subject or internal merits, is truly a portion of the national history; we may imitate it and print it in facsimile, but we can never exactly reproduce it; and as an historical document it should be carefully preserved.

A few lines later, Blades closes *The Enemies of Books* with a reminder that ". . . every book is a personal friend."

The future of books may depend simply on everyone who owns them. Books that are old today will have a future if we take care of each precious individual volume now. We can provide a future for new books by helping them age gracefully.

As book dealers, we may be entitled, or just expected, to pontificate on the future of books. We ask ourselves the question, and find that it brings us back to the relationship between books and dogs and the people who love both.

It's been said that dogs helped make us human, gave us the security to settle and think and sleep through the night and invent and create all the things we have come to call civilization. Some fine books have been written on the subject.

Human beings are always eager for improvement, in their things if not in themselves. We even "improve" dogs, for good and ill, because we have the know-how. By all means, build a better mousetrap. A terrier can take over when it fails.

Will we build a better book? There are already clever devices that deliver book content, and much anticipation. . . .

. . . and many more old books to find and clean and make whole again and place in good homes. As we see it, the electronic book is to the traditional book as the robotic dog is to the living, breathing canine. No doubt electronic books (and all book equivalents) are here to stay, and robotic dogs (with their "personality modules") are great fun, and may they flourish as the novelties they are. But neither will replace what it represents. Not while there are rags and rubbing alcohol, biscuits, walks, and tennis balls, and people who love books and dogs.

A MODEST GLOSSARY

Defined here are only the terms that appear in this book. More-comprehensive glossaries appear in many books, including some of those we recommend under "Suggested Reading."

On the Internet, we find the glossaries provided by Advanced Book Exchange (www.abebooks.com) and Trussel's EclectiCity (www.trussel.com; click on "Books & Collecting") especially useful and easy to use.

At abebooks.com, the extensive lexicon of book terms is supplemented by detailed guides on book sizes ("octavo," or 8vo, and its mates) and book conditions (what is meant by "near fine"? what is a "reading copy"?). And there's a good list of abbreviations commonly used in the book trade.

ADHESIVE   Any product that joins elements of a book together, such as liquid plastics; see also GLUE and PASTE.

ARCHIVAL QUALITY   The term connotes acid-free components and long-lasting protection.

BINDING   The cover materials that make a book whole. Also, the process of attaching a cover to the text block.

BLANK   A book page on which there is no printing, such as a printer's blank often found at the beginning of a book or a verso (left-hand page) at the end of a section of a book.

BOARDS   The front and back covers of a hardcover book; the stiff portions of a binding.

BONE FOLDER   An oblong tool with rounded edges, made of plastic or bone. It is used to make precise creases and in other book-related tasks.

BOOK DUMMY   A device that fills the gap created when a book is removed from a shelf. It helps keep remaining books upright. In library practice, the dummy usually identifies the book removed and its whereabouts.

BOOK WEIGHTS   Objects, commonly fabric-covered bricks, used to apply pressure to books during and after repair.

BOOKWORM   Insect larva that feeds on books, especially on paste. Also, a person who devours books.

BOUND   An adhesive-bound book is made to be of one piece; its text block and binding are glued together in the manufacturing process.

CASED   The cased book or case-bound book implies the conjoining of two parts (the pages inside, or contents, often called the text block, and the outside, or covers and spine).

CHIP, CHIPPING   A missing portion of a dust jacket or book page. The jacket or page so afflicted is said to be "chipped."

CLEANING GEL   A chemical product, usually containing a petroleum distillate, useful in cleaning and reviving book covers.

CONSERVATION   In contemporary book parlance, conservation includes preservation (see page 141) but requires that original materials be maintained.

COVERS   A book's boards, which comprise the front and back covers, and the spine.

DACHSHUND   The long-bodied, short-legged "badger dog" of German origin. The ultimate in intelligent companionship.

DOG-EAR, DOG-EARED   The turned-down corner of a book page.

DRY CLEANING PAD   A palm-sized, nonabrasive book-grooming tool, filled with ground Artgum, silicon, or similar tiny particles. Opaline is an old trade name for the product, so well-known that it has become all but synonymous with the pad, which is sold under various names.

EDGES   The three paper sides of a book: top, fore, and bottom.

EDGEWEAR   Catchall term referring to usually modest damage to a book's edges.

EMBOSSED, EMBOSSING   A decorative effect incorporating raised work.

ENDPAPERS   Double leaves (pages) common to modern books; one portion adheres to the inside of a book's cover (the paste-down); the other forms the flyleaf or free endpaper.

EPHEMERA   The plural of "emphemeron" (a short-lived insect) denotes usually paper articles, often related to a book or its author (such as promotional materials) or simply of sentimental value (letters, ticket stubs, playbills), which were not intended for long life.

FLYLEAF   See ENDPAPERS.

FOXED, FOXING   Refers to the discoloration, usually a yellowish brown, that appears on old paper.

FREE ENDPAPER   See ENDPAPERS.

GAUFFRED (or GOFFERED)   Describes book edges to which ridged or pleated decoration has been imparted by a heated tool onto gilt or silvered paper.

GILT   Gold of surpassing thinness, often used in lettering or applied as decoration.

GLASSINE   A thin, dense paper, either transparent or semitransparent, that inhibits the passage of air or other substances.

GLUE   An adhesive derived from animal products.

GRANGERIZE, GRANGERIZER   The art, or insult, of adding illustrations to a book, often with artwork removed from other books. The term derives from the eighteenth-century English clergyman James Granger. His *Biographical History of England* (1769) was issued with blank leaves for the purpose of extra-illustration.

GUTTER   The space created by the adjoining margins of facing pages.

HALF TITLE   The page preceding a book's title page, on which only the book's title appears.

HEAD   The top of a book, its spine or pages.

HINGES   The point where a book cover is joined to the text block.

INSET   A graphic device, such as an illustration or decoration, set within a larger space, such as a book cover.

LAMINATE   The glossy surface of many modern books; the process involves the bonding of layers of paper with resin and their compression under heat.

LOOSE   Said of a book page or signature when it is no longer attached to the book.

MARBLED, MARBLING   Refers to the patterns of swirls that decorate book paper (usually endpapers) or edges.

MELINEX   A polyester film; DuPont's Melinex 516 replaced Mylar for use in the graphic arts industry, including clear book jackets.

MILDEW   Growth, usually superficial and whitish in color, produced by fungi, most often of the families Erysiphaceae and Peronosporaceae. In book-related discussions, often used interchangeably with mold.

MOLD   A superficial growth, often with a woolly texture, produced by fungi of such orders as Mucorales. In book-related discussions, often used interchangeably with mildew.

MYLAR   The well-known DuPont polyester film that endures in a zillion clear book jackets. Its successor in the graphic arts industry is Melinex 516.

PASTE   An adhesive derived from plant products.

PETROLATUM   Petroleum jelly (Vaseline is a well-known trademark); useful as a solvent in book cleaning.

PRESERVATION   In terms of books or other media, preservation entails saving by reproduction and permits the destruction of original materials. A book may be torn apart, its contents digitized, photographed, or otherwise made available. That book may then be burned, yet it will have been "preserved."

RED ROT   A condition of overly dry leather books, in which the surface degenerates and flakes.

REMAINDER MARK   The ink mark, large or small, often red or black, found on a book's edges.

ROUGH-TRIMMED   See UNTRIMMED.

SIGNATURE   A unit of book pages made from a single folded sheet printed on both sides whose edges are cut to size on three sides. Signatures usually are comprised of 30 pages but can be 16, 8, or even 4 pages, depending on the size and thickness of the paper.

SILVERFISH   A member of the wingless insect order Thysanura; *Lepisma saccharina* is especially destructive to sized paper.

SIZED   Paper has been sized when it is treated with viscid or glutinous washes, which fill its pores to produce a uniform surface.

SPINE   The backbone of a book, this is the part of a book's cover between the side covers that most of us think of as "front" and "back."

SPRINKLED   The speckled effect of color, usually added to a book's edges.

SUNNED   Bleached, faded; often seen on the spines of books.

TAIL   The bottom of a book, its spine or pages.

TEXT BLOCK   The book's pages.

TRIM, TRIMMED   Refers to the condition of book edges. Indicates that pages are cut to uniform smoothness.

UNOPENED   Describes book pages in which the fore and top edges of succeeding pages have not been cut. Not always a fault.

UNTRIMMED   In reference to book edges, describes pages that are not cut to uniform smoothness. Sometimes called "rough-trimmed."

WRAPS   A paperback book's covers.

A BIBLIO LIST

In this short list of some of the less often used, but endlessly useful, compounds based on the Greek *biblion,* we have limited definitions to the purely secular. We welcome, and will reply to, all complaints from divinity students and Biblical scholars.

BIBLIOCLASM   The destruction or mutilation of books. The biblioclast must be hunted down and publicly humiliated.

BIBLIOGENESIS, BIBLIOGONY   The production of books.

BIBLIOGNOST   Someone with a deep knowledge of books; a bibliosoph.

BIBLIOKLEPT   A book thief.

BIBLIOLATRY   Extravagant devotion to books, or excessive concern for them. A bibliolater's lot is usually a happy one.

BIBLIOMANCY   Divination using books. Try it the Greek or Roman way, by consulting the works of Homer (*sortes Homericae*) and Virgil (*sortes Virgilianae*), mindful that it was probably the Romans to whom we owe the shape of modern books.

BIBLIOMANIA   The passion for collecting books. The happy sufferer is a bibliomane or bibliomaniac.

BIBLIOPEGY   Bookbinding, its art and craft. A practitioner is a bibliopegist.

BIBLIOPHAGY   The consumption of books. The bibliophage, or bibliophagist, devours books, preferably by avid reading. Beware the bibliophageous bug, such as the bookworm.

BIBLIOPHILE, BIBLIOPHILISM   A lover of books, a book collector; the love of books and book collecting.

BIBLIOPHOBIA   The hatred of books. A bibliophobe is someone to be helped, if you can endure it, or utterly shunned.

BIBLIOPOESY   The making of books (as distinct from "bookmaking").

BIBLIOPOLE   A book dealer, usually specializing in rare books. A person engaged in bibliopoly, or bibliopolism, is also called a bibliopolist.

BIBLIOSIS   The dread condition discovered during book sniffing, recognizable by a foul odor. Often treatable.

BIBLIOSOPH   Someone with a deep knowledge of books; a bibliognost.

BIBLIOTAPH   A person who keeps books hidden or locked away.

BIBLIOTHERAPY   The treatment of personal problems or some psychological disorders by the reading of selected books. A wise bibliotherapist may combine the treatment with cynotherapy, which employs the healing power of dogs.

BIBLIOTHETIC   Pertaining to the arrangement of books.

BIBLIOTICS   The study of written documents to ascertain authenticity or authorship.

SUGGESTED READING

The following recommendations, including many out-of-print titles, are just a sampling of the vast literature on the love of books, their care and history, and the people who make books the center of their lives. Some of these books are full of modern-day practicalities. Others are a change of time and place that provides inspiration, a bit of fun, and the stuff of good conversation.

Books
꿏

AHEARN, ALLEN AND PATRICIA. *Book Collecting 2000— A Comprehensive Guide*. New York: Putnam, 2000. Estimates the market values of first printings of about six thousand authors.

BAKER, NICHOLSON. *Double Fold: Libraries and the Assault on Paper*. New York: Random House, 2001. The policy of "destroying to preserve" and the fate of books, newspapers, and periodicals in America's libraries.

BASBANES, NICHOLAS A. *A Gentle Madness: Bibliophiles, Bibliomanes, and the Eternal Passion for Books.* New York: Henry Holt, 1995. A world history of book collecting and the mania it inspires.

―――――. *Patience and Fortitude: A Roving Chronicle of Book People, Book Places, and Book Culture.* New York: HarperCollins, 2001. The title takes the names of the beloved stone lions outside the New York Public Library's main branch on Fifth Avenue, and the lions would be proud to join on this chatty ramble.

BLADES, WILLIAM. *The Enemies of Books.* London: Truebner & Co., 1880. This book has been reprinted several times, and remains proof that among the things that never change are such hazards as water, pests, dust, and neglect. The second edition is recommended for the author's corrections and additions.

CARTER, JOHN. *ABC for Book Collectors (seventh edition).* New Castle: Oak Knoll Press, 1995. With corrections, additions, and an introduction by Nicolas Barker. An indispensable guide to collecting, the book industries, and the book trade.

COCKERELL, DOUGLAS. *Bookbinding and the Care of Books: A Handbook for Amateurs, Bookbinders and Librarians.* New York: Lyons Press, 1991. A favorite with many bookbinders to this day, by the foremost bookbinder of the early twentieth century; with an introduction by Jane Greenfield.

DARLING, WILL Y. *The Bankrupt Bookseller.* Edinburgh: Robert Grant & Son Ltd., 1947. Comprises *The Private Papers of a Bankrupt Bookseller* (1931) and *The Bankrupt Bookseller Speaks Again* (1938); with an introduction to the first common edition by Harold Forrester. "The book was begun as a jest," Forrester writes, "and the cream of the jest is that the author was neither a bookseller nor a bankrupt, and though he now owns two bookshops he is still, perhaps to his own surprise, not yet insolvent." Recommended for anyone fascinated by the life and work of a book dealer.

DONALDSON, GERALD. *Books: Their History, Art, Power, Glory, Infamy and Suffering According to Their Creators, Friends and Enemies.* New York: Van Nostrand Reinhold, 1981. An illustrated anthology, from the origin of the word *book* to surveys of the habits of bookshop browsers.

ELLIS, ESTELLE, CAROLINE SEEBOHM, AND CHRISTOPHER SIMON SYKES. *At Home with Books: How Book Lovers Live with and Care for Their Libraries.* New York: Random House, 1995. Wonderful illustrations.

FIELD, EUGENE. *The Love Affairs of a Bibliomaniac.* New York: Charles Scribner's Sons, 1896. With an introduction by the author's brother, Roswell Martin Field.

Pure balm for the book lover, in such chapters as "Baldness and Intellectuality," "On the Odors Which My Books Exhale," "The Luxury of Reading in Bed," and "The Malady Called Catalogitis."

FLAUBERT, GUSTAVE. *Bibliomania: A Tale*. Emmaus: Rodale Press, 1954. The author of *Madame Bovary* was only fourteen when he wrote this study of the notorious monk and bibliomaniac Don Vincente. This edition is illustrated by Arthur Wragg.

GOLDSTONE, LAWRENCE AND NANCY. *Slightly Chipped: Footnotes in Booklore*. New York: St. Martin's Press, 1999. The enchanted lives of avid book collectors, by the authors of the entertaining *Used and Rare: Travels in the Book World*.

GREENFIELD, JANE. *ABC of Bookbinding: An Illustrated Glossary of Terms for Collectors and Conservators*. New Castle: Oak Knoll Press, 1997. All the definitions you'll ever need, and more than seven hundred line drawings.

———. *Books: Their Care and Repair*. New York: The H. W. Wilson Company, 1983. Straightforward instruction, with many line drawings.

———. *The Care of Fine Books*. New York: Lyons & Burford, 1988. A standard manual on conservation and restoration.

HUTTON, LAURENCE. *From the Books of.* New York: Harper and Brothers, 1892. Selections from the author's library of seventeenth- and eighteenth-century literature focus on "oddities and curiosities." Especially good reading is the chapter on "Grangerism and the Grangerites."

HUXFORD, BOB AND SHARON. *Huxford's Old Book Value Guide.* Paducah: Collector Books, 2001. The thirteenth edition, which lists twenty-five thousand books and their market values, concentrates on titles in the $10 to $15 range.

JACKSON, H. J. *Marginalia: Readers Writing in Books.* New Haven: Yale University Press, 2001. The history and practice of a habit that is as revelatory to some as it is repugnant to others.

MCBRIDE, BILL, compiled by. *A Pocket Guide to the Identification of First Editions.* West Hartford: McBride/Publisher, 2000. The sixth edition of the indispensable pocket-sized guide, expanded to more than thirty-seven hundred publishers. Available, along with the book below and other books on books, at the publisher's Web site: www.jumpingfrog.com.

———. *Points of Issue: A Compendium of Points of Issue of Books by 19th–20th Century Authors.* West Hartford: McBride/Publishers, 1996. The third edition elucidates more than fifteen hundred points relevant to

American and British editions from 1850 to the present. Includes dust jacket points and faux book club firsts.

MORLEY, CHRISTOPHER, compiled by. *Ex Libris.* Philadelphia: J. B. Lippincott, 1936. An anthology originally issued as a souvenir of the First National Book Fair (November 1936) and drawn from unexpected sources, including contemporary newspaper columns and bookseller catalogs.

NEWTON, A. EDWARD. *The Amenities of Book-Collecting and Kindred Affections.* Boston: The Atlantic Monthly Press, 1918. The author's adventures in America and Europe, with observations on authors still famous and many now forgotten.

————. *A Magnificent Farce and Other Diversions of a Book-Collector.* Boston: The Atlantic Monthly Press, 1921. Essays as opinionated as they are entertaining.

PETROSKI, HENRY. *The Book on the Bookshelf.* New York: Alfred A. Knopf, 1999. An enlightening history of shelving and storage of all sorts, with much information on bookbinding and related topics.

POWERS, ALAN. *Living with Books.* San Francisco: SOMA Books, 1999. A visual treat, with ideas on how to decorate with books and how to provide fine storage for your books.

ROSTENBERG, LEONA, AND MADELEINE B. STERN. *Between Boards: New Thoughts on Old Books.* Montclair: Allanheld, Osmun & Co./London: Abner Schram Ltd., 1978. The world of antiquarian bookselling and collecting, by two leading practitioners and dachshund devotees.

————. *Old Books in the Old World: Reminiscences of Book Buying Abroad.* New Castle: Oak Knoll, 1996. The authors' European book-buying expeditions between 1947 and 1957.

————. *Old Books, Rare Friends: Two Literary Sleuths and Their Shared Passion.* New York: Doubleday, 1997.

SIEGEL, DAVID S. AND SUSAN. *The Used Book Lover's Guides.* Yorktown Heights: Book Hunter Press. Seven regional titles (New England, Mid Atlantic States, South Atlantic States, Midwest, Central/Western States, Pacific Coast States, and Canada) survey eight thousand used, out-of-print, and antiquarian dealers. Updated routinely, the guides are available in print editions and by online subscription (www.bookhunterpress.com). Use them to plan a travel itinerary, from bookshop to bookshop, or to find dealers who specialize in your favorite subjects.

WILCOX, ANNIE TREMMEL. *A Degree of Mastery: A Journey Through Book Arts Apprenticeship.* Minneapolis: New Rivers Press, 1999. The author recounts her study of bookbinding and paper conservation at the University of Iowa Center for the Book.

Two old-fashioned novels portray bookselling as we often wish it remained today. Both capture the imagined romance of the trade and are enlivened by a memorable Irish terrier: Christopher Morley's *Parnassus on Wheels* and *The Haunted Bookshop*. Published early in the twentieth century, both have gone through numerous editions, and were reprinted as recently as 2000 (Pleasantville: Akadine Press). You may already know the novels' book dealer, Roger Mifflin, by a passage often quoted: "When you sell a man a book, you don't sell him twelve ounces of paper and ink and glue—you sell him a whole new life."

Two contemporary mystery novels are irresistible to anyone who loves books. John Dunning introduced his book-besotted detective, Cliff Janeway, in *Booked to Die* (New York: Scribner, 1992) and brought him back in *The Bookman's Wake* (New York: Scribner, 1995).

Especially interested in books about books? Visit www.oakknollpress.com for more than 850 titles on the subject.

A Useful Periodical
✤

Book Source Monthly. Essays, opinion, and news of book sales, auctions, dealers, and other indispensables. Available by subscription (PO Box 567, Cazenovia, NY 13035-0567; telephone and fax 315/655-8499; www.booksourcemonthly.com) and from some newsagents and bookstores.

Especially for Children
❧

BROOKFIELD, KAREN. *Book.* New York: Dorling Kindersley, 2000. Profusely illustrated "Eyewitness" series guide to the history of books, writing, and printing. Appropriate for readers as young as grade 2 students, and a handsome reference for all book lovers.

KALMAN, BOBBIE. *How a Book Is Published.* New York: Crabtree Publishing (Crabapples series), 1996. From concept to finished product, the functions of editors and illustrators, and other facts for budding authors. For ages four to eight.

LIDDLE, MATTHEW. *Make Your Own Book: A Complete Kit.* Philadelphia: Running Press, 1993. A boxed set, with supplies and a Bookmaking Handbook to explain how to write and produce a thirty-two-page book.

ZIEGLER, ROBERT G. *Homemade Books to Help Kids Cope: An Easy-to-Learn Technique for Parents and Professionals.* Washington, D.C.: American Psychological Association, 1992. The art and importance of personalized books, and their therapeutic role.

SUPPLIERS

The suppliers listed below may specialize in serving library and other institutional customers, but they all cater to individual customers. Don't hesitate to ask questions (except of the one supplier whose exception-to-the-rule role we note below); we've found telephone salespeople and their Internet counterparts willing to explain how to use their products to best effect and helpful in selecting the right product for specific tasks.

Many of the supplier Web sites post not only the complete product line in searchable form, but also such attractions as discontinued stock at reduced prices, video tours of their manufacturing and shipping facilities, e-mail notification of new products, newsletters, and all kinds of advice. Sophisticated and secure online ordering, order tracking, and privacy policies are the norm.

These are the companies to query for archival-quality clear book jacket covers, professional-quality adhesives and solvents, tapes for every imaginable book-related use, all the appropriate tools, and a host of ingenious gadgets.

Many also sell appliances such as small vacuum cleaners with nozzles designed for book cleaning. Some of the library and office furnishings and equipment are ideal in the home for work or study. Accessories and cases for storing, preserving, and organizing videocassettes and audiocassettes, slides and photographic negatives, CDs, and DVDs may make your life easier. There are all kinds of bookends and other devices to help keep bookshelves tidy. You might consider the wide variety of archival-quality document boxes, binders, and other containers that safeguard magazines, fragile paper materials, photographs, and other ephemera.

As of this writing, conventional printed catalogs were still available from all the suppliers listed here.

BRODART
www.brodart.com
> Brodart Order Center, PO Box 3037, Williamsport, PA 17705
> Telephone (888) 820-4377 for orders
> Fax (800) 283-6087 for orders
> supplies@brodart.com for general information
> supplies.productinfo@brodart.com for product information

Thousands of products for libraries, bookstores, and offices. The array of book jacket covers includes a line of fine archival-quality covers that are easy to use. Brodart offers its "Basic Book Repair" and "Book Jacket Cover Selection Guide" in both print and online versions.

CONSERVATION RESOURCES INTERNATIONAL, LLC
www.conservationresources.com
>   8000-H Forbes Place, Springfield, VA 22151
>   Telephone (800) 634-6932 or (703) 321-7730
>   Fax (703) 321-0629
>   criusa@conservationresources.com

This company's line includes highly specialized conservation products and archival storage items and everything you need to preserve natural history artifacts and textiles.

DEMCO
www.demco.com
>   PO Box 7488, Madison, WI 53707-7488
>   Telephone (800) 356-1200 for orders, (800) 962-4463 for customer service, (608) 241-1799 for customer service from outside the United States
>   Fax (800) 245-1329
>   custserv@demco.com
>   international@demco.com for help with orders shipped outside the United States.

Demco has a wide range of products for libraries (its first library pocket was marketed in 1905), schools, and offices.

GAYLORD BROS.
www.gaylordmart.com
>   PO Box 4901, Syracuse, NY 13221-4901
>   Telephone (800) 634-6307 in the United States, (800) 841-5854 in Canada, (315) 457-5070 extension 287 from other countries

Fax (800) 272-3412 in the United States, (800) 615-3779 in Canada, (315) 453-5030 from other countries

customerservice@gaylord.com

The company offers an enormous selection of book- and paper-related products. Gaylord's "Pathfinder" series of pamphlets on various aspects of preservation and archival storage of paper, photographs, and textiles includes one on introductory book repair. The concise guides can be downloaded from the Web site or requested in print form.

HIGHSMITH INC.
www.highsmith.com
> W5527 Highway 106, PO Box 800, Fort Atkinson, WI 53538-0800
> Telephone (800) 558-2110
> Fax (800) 835-2329
> service@highsmith.com

Ask for Highsmith's helpful "Care & Repair: Book-Saving Techniques" booklet, which retails for $5.30. A feature of the Web site is a glimpse of the company's art collection; commissioned artworks have graced the library products catalogs since 1978.

TALAS
www.talasonline.com
> 568 Broadway (just north of Prince Street), New York, NY 10012
> Telephone (212) 219-0770
> Fax (212) 219-0735
> info@talasonline.com

Given the staff's level of expertise, what a pity that company policy is not to give advice! The Talas showroom in Manhattan's SoHo neighborhood of galleries and good shopping and dining is open to the public. Come with your shopping list finalized, but not with an injured book and questions about its repair. Or drop by to peruse the bulletin board, which displays book professionals' business cards and news of book-related events. The nearest subway stop is Prince Street.

The Talas Web site details products intended for professional-level conservation, presentation, and restoration, and few of the items are useful to the tyro. If and when you master any of the book arts, however, you will find the Talas stock an important resource. The company issues a printed catalog, for which there may be a charge.

UNIVERSITY PRODUCTS
www.universityproducts.com
517 Main Street, PO Box 101, Holyoke, MA 01041-0101
Telephone (800) 628-1912
Fax (800) 532-9281
custserve@universityproducts.com

The site is a gateway to a range of products and information resources—librarysuppliers.com, archivalsupppliers.com, archivalware.com, and archival.net—for conservation, restoration, preservation, and exhibition.

VERNON LIBRARY SUPPLIES INC.
www.vernlib.com
2851 Cole Court, Norcross, GA 30071
Telephone (800) 878-0253 or (770) 446-1128 in the Atlanta area

Fax (800) 466-1165 or (770) 447-0165 in the Atlanta area
vernon@vernlib.com

There are a variety of book jacket covers, mending tapes,
and other book-care products from which to choose, as well
as archival storage containers of all sorts.

MISCELLANEOUS RESOURCES Miniature handheld
vacuum cleaners are indispensable in cleaning books and
their shelves. Hair dryers, especially travel-sized models
that restrict airflow and direct it more or less precisely, are
useful in loosening price tags and other anti-adhesive
tasks. Some of the suppliers listed above market small
vacuum cleaners; we've also found them offered on and
off the Internet from such merchants as Sears, Home
Depot, and automotive suppliers. For a travel-sized hair
dryer, your best bet may be your local all-purpose drug-
store or department store. Or ask personnel at a barber-
shop or beauty salon for advice on which make and model
give the best temperature and airflow control.

THE BOOK ARTS
AND CONSERVATION ON
THE INTERNET

Whether you're motivated by simple curiosity or the need to preserve a beloved book or other paper-based treasure, the organizations below can help. They are good places to start if you think book care might become your new hobby or when you begin to wonder if the book arts would suit you as a new career.

In addition to promoting awareness of the book crafts and educating the book-loving public, these groups' Web sites can inform you on the nuts and bolts of everything from papermaking to bookbinding, marbling, calligraphy, and that grand old passion, letterpress printing. The Web sites invariably feature links throughout the book world, and can put you in touch with professional bookbinders and other specialists. Many have online exhibits, and most have extensive texts for reference.

In the real world, many offer lectures and exhibitions, membership programs, referrals on book-related questions, and training courses that range from the rudimentary to the exotic.

Remember that your *Yellow Pages* may list book-binders, and your local bookseller may be able to advise you when you need professional book care services.

THE BOOK ARTS WEB

www.philobiblon.com

The comprehensive links page can involve you in a philosophic discussion on the definition of a book, connect you with meta sites for book searches, or put you in touch with a French family of professional gold beaters (in the gold leaf business only since 1834). There's an online gallery, with links to more such exhibits of book arts around the world, and an extensive archive of LISTSERV postings from which you may cull just the fact or opinion you want.

THE CANADIAN BOOKBINDERS AND BOOK ARTISTS GUILD

www.cbbag.ca

> 176 John Street, Suite 309, Toronto, ON M5T 1X5
> Telephone (416) 581-1071
> Fax (416) 581-1053
> cbbag@web.net

The site's online exhibition is available with French-language commentary.

THE CENTER FOR BOOK ARTS

www.centerforbookarts.org

> 28 West 27th Street, third floor, New York, NY 10001
> Telephone (212) 481-0295
> info@centerforbookarts.org

Open to the public on weekdays and Saturday, the center has classes and workshops of all sorts, from the traditional crafts to new perspectives on the book. Such subjects as basic book repair, decorative gilding, miniature books, and Japanese bookbinding are taught.

THE CONSERVATION CENTER FOR ART AND HISTORIC ARTIFACTS
www.ccaha.org
  264 South 23rd Street, Philadelphia, PA 19103
  Telephone (215) 545-0613
  Fax (215) 735-9313
  ccaha@ccaha.org

The nonprofit conservation laboratory treats all kinds of historic paper-based items, from rare books to maps and prints to wallpaper, as well as parchment and papyrus.

CONSERVATION ONLINE
palimpsest.stanford.edu

CoOL is a project of the Preservation Department of Stanford University Libraries. Of special interest, under the "Conservation Topics" heading, are the "General Public" link and those on mold and a wide range of book- and conservation-related suppliers and services.

THE GUILD OF BOOK WORKERS
palimpsest.stanford.edu/byorg/gbw
  521 Fifth Avenue, New York, NY 10175

The nonprofit guild has a global membership of more than a thousand experts in all the book arts. To be put in touch with a recommended binder or other professional, send your request in writing to the Fifth Avenue address.

NORTHEAST DOCUMENT CONSERVATION CENTER
www.nedcc.org
>   100 Brookstone Square, Andover, MA 01810-1494
>   Telephone (978) 470-1010
>   Fax (978) 475-6021
>   nedcc@nedcc.org

Learn about preservation and conservation policies and methods pertinent to every situation, from private collections to museums. The vast site, with extensive coverage of book and paper preservation, has exceptionally fine links.

TRUSSEL'S ECLECTICITY
www.trussel.com

The site's "Books & Book Collecting" section connects you to everything from author bibliographies and pseudonym dictionaries to sources of old and new books and links relevant to all book-related matters, from the most fanciful to the most practical.

BOOK ARTS STUDIES

These are some of the institutions that can help you pursue formal education in the field, from intensive workshops and seminars to postgraduate degrees.

AMERICAN ACADEMY OF BOOKBINDING
www.ahhaa.org
>   PO Box 1590, Telluride, CO 81435
>   Telephone (970) 728-3886
>   Fax (970) 728-9709
>   staff@ahhaa.org

A year-round schedule of classes serving adults and children; bookbinding is just the beginning of these eclectic offerings.

THE CENTER FOR BOOK ARTS
www.centerforbookarts.org
>   28 West 27th Street, third floor, New York, NY 10001
>   Telephone (212) 481-0295
>   info@centerforbookarts.org

Courses on all facets of the field, from basic repair and decorative gilding to miniature books, Japanese bookbinding, and printing.

COLUMBIA COLLEGE CHICAGO/CENTER FOR BOOK AND PAPER ARTS
www.bookandpaper.org
    1104 South Wabash Avenue, Chicago, IL 60605
    Telephone (312) 344-6630
    Fax (312) 344-8082
    bookandpaper@popmail.colum.edu

Classes for the general public are offered, as well as courses for college credit; all the basics are covered, including "Book Structure" and "Unique Bindings."

MINNESOTA CENTER FOR BOOK ARTS
www.mnbookarts.org
    1011 Washington Avenue South, Suite 100, Minneapolis, MN 55415
    Telephone (612) 215-2520
    Fax (612) 215-2520
    mcba@mnbookarts.org

Lectures, master classes, interdisciplinary workshops, exhibits—all the traditional crafts are taught and practiced.

NORTH BENNET STREET SCHOOL
www.nbss.org
    39 North Bennet Street, Boston, MA 02113
    Telephone (617) 227-0155
    admission@nbss.org

Bookbinding courses are regular features of the curriculum.

OREGON COLLEGE OF ART & CRAFT
www.ocac.edu
    8245 SW Barnes Road, Portland, OR 97225
    Telephone (503) 297-5544
    admissions@ocac.edu

The Book Arts Department offers a range of basic courses and special-interest workshops.

PENLAND SCHOOL OF CRAFTS
www.penland.org
    PO Box 37, Penland, NC 28765
    Telephone (828) 765-2359
    Fax (828) 765-7389
    office@penland.org

Workshops in the Blue Ridge Mountains focus on book and paper crafts.

RARE BOOK SCHOOL
www.virginia.edu/oldbooks
    114 Alderman Library, University of Virginia, Charlottesville, VA 22901-2498
    Telephone (804) 924-8851
    Fax (804) 924-8824
    oldbooks@virginia.edu

Five-day courses on the history of books and printing are scheduled throughout the year.

THE SAN FRANCISCO CENTER FOR THE BOOK
www.sfcb.org
>   300 DeHaro Street, San Francisco, CA 94103
>   Telephone (415) 565-0545
>   info@sfcb.org

Programs include those sponsored by member organizations, The Hand Bookbinders of California and the Pacific Center for the Book Arts.

UNIVERSITY OF IOWA CENTER FOR THE BOOK
www.uiowa.edu/~ctrbook.
>   216 North Hall, Iowa City, IA 52242
>   Telephone (319) 335-0438
>   Center-for-the-book@uiowa.edu

Studies cover the history and subjective impact of the book as well as bookbinding and the creation of new books.

WELLS COLLEGE BOOK ARTS CENTER
www.wells.edu/bkarts/bkarts1.htm
>   Aurora, NY 13026
>   Telephone (315) 364-3266
>   bookartscenter@wells.edu

Emphasis at the upstate New York institution is on the making of books and fine bindings.

AN INTERNET MISCELLANY

www.beachreader.com

Tabletop and tripod accessories from Crispus Enterprises help you read or write comfortably while standing or sitting on the beach or in any other unconventional setting.

www.booksalefinder.com

At Book Sale Finder, lists of book sales, from library sales to antiquarian book fairs, are just a click away, and organized by U.S. state and Canadian province. The site offers an e-mail newsletter, too.

www.elmers.com

Great glue facts—why does glue remain fluid in a bottle? why is Elmer's white? how did the bull Elmer become the product's representative? Information on using Elmer's Glue-All and Krazy Glue. Great stuff for kids, too.

www.folusa.com

Friends of Libraries U.S.A., a membership organization based in Philadelphia, can help you if you want to help your local library. Books for Babies, which promotes reading, is just one of their worthwhile activities.

www.geocities.com/Athens/Olympus/4369/Bookplate/ introd.htm

The Art of the Ex Libris, with large-scale illustrations that show good detail, tells the history of the bookplate from the fifteenth century, and discusses bookplate collecting.

www.levenger.com

Levenger's "Tools for Serious Readers" available on the Web site, and in the printed catalog, range from lamps and light fixtures to book stands, lap desks, and magnifiers.

www.planet-typography.com

For aficionados of printing history, typography and typographers, and typefaces. Downloadable typefaces available include non-Latin fonts.

www.tappi.org/paperu

The history of paper and its uses and recycling, in a question-and-answer format that young people will find entertaining. With a lot of good information on the role of trees.

www.3m.com

History, development, and uses galore for some nine hundred pressure-sensitive adhesives, including the ubiquitous Scotch brand tapes. Good reading throughout the site, including the story of how an entire product line got "stuck" with the Scotch name.

A BIBLIOMANIAC'S
MANHATTAN MILE

There are always books and manuscripts on view, in permanent collections and special exhibitions, and bookshops, too, in all the institutions along Fifth Avenue's Museum Mile. But New York City has what we consider a Bibliomaniac's Mile to rival any in the world.

The itinerary can be done in one busy day. For more browsing time at each stop, divide the route in two, making a southern circuit one day and a northern expedition the other, both from a distinctive address in Midtown.

If you're a visitor to New York City, or a resident in need of a holiday without airport hassle, check into an unusual boutique hotel on the East Side.

The Library Hotel (299 Madison Avenue at 41st Street; telephone 212/983-4500 or toll free 877/793-7323; fax 212/499-9099; www.libraryhotel.com; reservations@libraryhotel.com) dedicates each of its ten floors to one of the major categories of the Dewey Decimal System: Social Sciences, Languages, Math and Science, Technology, The Arts, Literature, History, General Knowledge,

Philosophy, or Religion. Each bedroom—there are six per floor—is "individually adorned with a collection of art and [thirty to forty] books relevant to one distinctive topic" within the floor's category. On the General Knowledge floor, for example, Room 1000.001 is "Libraries," Room 1000.003, "Encyclopedias." Book into Room 800.005 on the Literature level, and you'll sleep among "Fairy Tales." On other floors are rooms devoted to dinosaurs, Germanic religion, zoology, ethics, Asian history, architecture, and love.

Facilities in keeping with the hotel's theme include a Poetry Garden and a Writer's Den, each with a terrace.

From the hotel, stroll south (downtown) on Madison Avenue to an office building between 38th and 39th Streets. On the fourth floor is the headquarters of the American Kennel Club (260 Madison Avenue; telephone 212/696-8245 for the library; www.akc.org; library@ akc.org). Your destination is the library, open weekdays only (except holidays).

Founded in 1934 with some fifty books, the AKC collection now has some seventeen thousand noncirculating volumes. Ask for research assistance, or sit and read to your heart's delight: issues of the *AKC Gazette* from 1889 to the present and other U.S. and foreign periodicals, stud books from all over the world, and books on individual breeds and their pursuits, art, literature, and history.

Be sure to look at one of the bookplates designed for the library by Edwin Megargee in 1936 (it's still used today). Among rare books you might want to admire is Skinner's *The Dog and the Sportsman* (1845), acclaimed as the first book of its kind published in America, or Caius's epochal *De Canibus Britannicis* (1570).

Continue south another two blocks, where across the avenue stands the Morgan Library (29 East 36th Street; telephone 212/685-0610; www.morganlibrary.org). Financier J. Pierpont Morgan began his collection of rare books and manuscripts in 1890. The collection spans ten centuries—papyri, medieval and Renaissance manuscripts, printed books (three Gutenberg Bibles, the manuscript of *A Christmas Carol* by Charles Dickens, Thoreau's journals), examples of bookbinding from as far back as the seventh century. Also on view in the Renaissance-style original library, designed by Charles McKim, are autograph scores, ancient Near Eastern seals, drawings and prints from the fourteenth through the twentieth centuries.

For refreshments, there's the Morgan Court Café. The Morgan Library Shop stocks choice books, including many about books, and exhibition catalogs; it's accessible directly from Madison Avenue, between 36th and 37th streets, without paying museum admission. The Morgan is open Tuesday through Sunday (closed holidays).

From the Morgan, continue downtown on Madison Avenue. On the southeast corner of 35th Street, there's The Complete Traveller Bookstore (199 Madison Avenue; telephone 212/685-9007), with as many as ten thousand travel books, most of them old, in an attractive setting where you'll enjoy browsing.

When you come to 33rd Street, notice the street sign: the block between Madison and Park Avenue is also known as Sholom Aleichem Place. The writer's works are among those you can find at the Jewish Book Center of the Workmen's Circle (45 East 33rd Street; telephone 212/889-6800; www.jewishbookcenter.org), which stocks some two thousand Yiddish titles.

Follow Madison Avenue downtown, to Madison Square Park. Stop by the popular dog run, or take a moment to amuse the squirrels. Then pick up Broadway on the park's southern end, at 23rd Street, and continue south.

Your next stop is the Strand Book Store (828 Broadway, at 12th Street; telephone 212/473-1452; www.strand books.com; strand@strandbooks.com), open daily and a fixture on the New York scene since 1927, when it opened on 4th Avenue, which was for decades the city's beloved Book Row.

The main store, entered at street level, advertises eight miles of books. The rare books are on the third floor, reached by an elevator you'll find in the lobby of the office building entrance; it's to the left (uptown side) as you face the Strand's street entrance.

The rare book department, probably the largest in the city, offers books in all price ranges, from under $10 to many thousands of dollars. The selection of books about books is especially large and varied.

Before heading back uptown from the massive Strand, you might stop in at intimate Alabaster Bookshop (122 4th Avenue; 212/982-3550; alabastr@hotmail.com), where books on New York City are among the specialties. It's right around the corner from the Strand, and like the larger store, usually has bargain books out front.

If you're covering the Bibliomaniac's Mile in one day, this is the time to trade the very best in modern urban rapid transit—walking—for a bus (northbound M1 or M2, both of which stop along 4th Avenue). Or walk north to Union Square for refreshments or a bag of farm produce or homemade cookies (at this writing, the open-air Greenmarket operates on Monday, Wednesday, Friday, and Saturday) before boarding the subway (uptown train 6 to 51st Street and Lexington Avenue or train 4 or 5 to 59th Street and Lexington) or the bus (uptown M1, M2, and M3 stop on Park Avenue South).

Your destination is Bauman Rare Books (535 Madison Avenue, between 54th and 55th streets; telephone 212/751-0011; www.baumanrarebooks.com; brb@bauman rarebooks.com). This is the firm's main New York gallery; there's a second at the Waldorf-Astoria (301 Park Avenue), as well as a shop in Philadelphia.

Bauman combines exceptional stock and elegant premises. Treasures in stock in the fall of 2001 included a rare first edition of *Pride and Prejudice* ($60,000); an early octavo of Audubon's *Quadrupeds of North America* ($18,000); a first of Conan Doyle's *The Hound of Baskervilles* ($6,200), with Sidney Paget illustrations; and an autographed photograph of Satchel Paige ($750). There are always wonderful children's books to admire— perhaps first editions of *Charlotte's Web*, Dr. Seuss classics, or *Peter Rabbit*. Be sure to ask for a copy of the Bauman catalog, with scrupulous detail on each offering and fine illustrations.

When you leave Bauman, "skibble"—as the object of

our last stop would express it—over to Fifth Avenue and Central Park South (59th Street) and the residence of one of New York City's great literary characters. On the Plaza Hotel's lobby level, in the south corridor adjacent to the Palm Court, hangs Hilary Knight's 1964 portrait of Kay Thompson's Eloise. A moment or two with Eloise, and her pug Weenie, ought to invigorate you for another round of book shopping.

INDEX

DATE DUE

The Joint Free Public Library
of
Morristown and Morris Township
1 Miller Road
Morristown, New Jersey 07960